Praise for

Sincerely, Katherine.

"One of the most sacred experiences a human being can navigate during their lifetime is a deep communion with their true self. This is far from an easy task. Katherine Dudtschak is a shining example of courage and authenticity as she redefined the notion of true leadership along the way in both her personal and professional life. Her story might not be yours, but don't be fooled, its lessons are universally *ours*."

SOPHIE GRÉGOIRE TRUDEAU, global speaker and bestselling author of *Closer Together*

"*Sincerely, Katherine.* is not just a memoir—it is a masterclass in courage, authenticity, and leadership. Katherine Dudtschak's words are not just a personal story—they are a call to action. *Sincerely, Katherine.* reminds us that when one person finds their voice and speaks their truth, it creates space for all of us to grow, to listen, and to evolve together. This book is a tender and transformative contribution to a more compassionate world."

DR. ROBYNE HANLEY-DAFOE, award-winning author of *Calm Within the Storm* and *Stress Wisely*

"*Sincerely, Katherine.* is a heartfelt story of Katherine Dudtschak's incredible personal journey mixed with life lessons and leadership perspectives for the future. I certainly appreciate how hard it is to share one's personal journey so publicly in the hope of making life better for others, as Katherine has in this book. She shares her life experiences so that others can gain a deeper understanding that while there may be differences among us, together we can move toward a brighter future based on kindness, inclusivity, and positive change."

PHIL FONTAINE, Indigenous Canadian leader and former National Chief of the Assembly of First Nations

"I have only ever known Katherine Dudtschak as the strong, inspiring woman that she is today. This book revealed so much I had not known about the life, challenges, and insights that unlocked the woman who never ceases to impress me. I highly recommend *Sincerely, Katherine.* for not only Katherine's generous sharing of her experience, but also her reflections on how inclusive leadership can have a fundamental impact on individuals, organizations, and society."

ANTHONY OSTLER, president and CEO of the Canadian Bankers Association and proud parent of two gender-affirmed children

"Katherine Dudtschak's story is inspiring and motivational. She is one of the bravest people that I know. Her insights and lived experiences will hopefully help others on their own journeys of self-realization and fulfillment. I am very proud and fortunate to call Katherine a friend and a tireless leader in our communities."

AL STRATHDEE, mayor of the Town of St. Marys and childhood friend

"Katherine Dudtschak powerfully and elegantly cuts through delusions and gently uses her genius to engage us into a new state of thought. Prepare yourself for a delicately written journey that will transform your soul into a timeless union of understanding sovereign boundaries and conscious interconnectedness. Katherine makes us sit up and realize how accessible compassion and empathy can stagger us into a deepseated look at our own lives."

PATRICIA K GAGIC, international artist, author, and founder of the Karmic Art Academy

"Katherine Dudtschak's story is a triumph of courage, authenticity, and love. Her life is a testament to living boldly and embracing every part of who you are."

COLLEEN JOHNSTON, philanthropist and former CFO of TD Bank

"It is a rare privilege in one's lifetime to meet a being as courageous, compassionate, and visionary as Katherine Dudtschak. She doesn't just speak of leadership—she embodies it. Her journey reflects a luminous form of wisdom, one that seeks harmony between the human spirit, others, nature, and the intelligent machines we have created."

DR. DELPHINE LE SERRE, founder and president of EdHu2050

"Katie's courage to be true to herself and to share her story has already impacted thousands of lives.

"Her mission to create a kinder, and more compassionate and inclusive world at home and at work is touching people's hearts and minds deeply. Her story has the power to make our world a better place for everyone.

"I am so proud of her. I can only imagine how incredibly proud our mom and dad would be. The thought brings tears to my eyes.

"We love you, Katie. Keep being you."

MONA CAMPBELL, Katherine Dudtschak's sister

Sincerely,

KATHERINE DUDTSCHAK

PAGE TWO

Katherine.

Life, Gender,
Inclusivity, and
Leadership for
the Future

Cataloguing in publication information is available from Library and Archives Canada.
ISBN 978-1-77458-692-1 (paperback)
ISBN 978-1-77458-633-4 (ebook)

Page Two
pagetwo.com

PAGE TWO™ is a trademark owned by Page Two Strategies Inc., and is used under licence by authorized licencees

Cover and interior design by Jennifer Lum
Cover photos by Sara Kardooni
Interior photos courtesy of the author
Printed and bound in Canada by Friesens
Distributed in Canada by Raincoast Books
Distributed in the US and internationally by Macmillan

26 27 28 29 30   5 4 3 2 1

sincerelykatherine.com

Contents

Modus vivendi:
a rhythm and way of being in the world

It is quite simple—nothing that is meant for you
will ever get away. Love deeply, and without the need
to possess or own; let beautiful connections pass through you
without attachment; slam your heart into the people and
places and things that ignite something deep inside of
your soul, and I promise, I promise: the right things will stay.
You will never lose what is for you.

*If you're brave enough to leave behind everything
familiar and comforting and set out on a truth seeking
journey either internally or externally, and if you are truly
willing to regard everything that happens to you on that
journey as a clue, and if you accept everyone you meet
along the way as a teacher, and if you are prepared most of all
to face and forgive some of the most difficult realities about
yourself, then the truth will not be withheld from you.*

ELIZABETH GILBERT, *Eat Pray Love*

Author's Note

THIS BOOK CONTAINS events and conversations that occurred over several decades, as far back as when I was a child. To the best of my ability, I have recounted the events, locales, and conversations within from my memories of them and have tried to include all credit where it is due. Any discrepancies and inaccuracies are my own. The interviews and meetings I mention in the book also stem from my recollections. I have retold them in a way that evokes the feeling and meaning of what was said, and in all instances, the essence of the dialogue is accurate.

This book includes many individuals who have been part of my journey and have impacted me deeply. In some cases, I share their full or just first name, with their permission, and in other cases, I have changed their name or not used it at all. I have done this out of love, respect, and privacy. I am deeply honoured and privileged to have had thousands of individuals touch me and shape me along the way, and I live each day in deep respect and appreciation of each and all, including those I have yet to meet.

Introduction

*When you see what you're here for, the world begins
to mirror your purpose in a magical way. It's almost
as if you suddenly find yourself on a stage in a play
that was written expressly for you.*

BETTY SUE FLOWERS

THIS STORY has been unfolding for many, many years—
for millions of years. It's taken 13.8 billion years to
create this exact moment in time in the universe; 4.5 billion years for our beautiful planet to reach this moment. Our
choice, my choice, is to embrace this moment with love, hope,
joy, freedom, and spirit, because the alternative is not really an
alternative. I know in the core of my soul that we as humans
possess a unique gift—the ability to be transformative, to *be*
in the most beautiful way; the ability to learn and iterate, to
collaborate and build from a place of presence, kindness, and
nurturance. From love.

This story, this letter, tells of my journey to know and
embrace myself, including affirming my gender as a woman,
as Katherine or Katie. While this took decades to unfold, and I

didn't affirm my gender until I was fifty years old, throughout the book I refer to myself as Katherine or Katie and use she/her pronouns. I decided to do so for my own and others' emotional well-being. On the inside, in my heart and mind, I have always been Katherine or Katie. You will not see references to my old name, or deadname. I have no regrets in life. I have complete love and acceptance of my life journey, of my family, friends, and colleagues.

While I use the term "transgender" in this writing, it's not a label I subscribe to. I'm a woman who affirmed her gender. I found and embraced my essence, including the unique mix of abilities, life experiences, genes, and feminine and masculine traits that have formed me and how I interact with the world.

Although my journey had always been happening, I really knew I was on it the day I stood in front of a poster about gender inclusivity in the hallway of my daughter's dorm. At that moment, I saw myself and something shifted for me. This day marked the beginning of a conscious journey that would transcend gender and take me to a much deeper place of essence and soul.

But no one else would have seen me in that poster. At the time, I had a masculine name and male appearance. I was one of Canada's most senior banking executives. My responsibilities included supporting and leading more than twenty-five thousand highly skilled advisors who served over fifteen million clients across Canada and the Caribbean.

I was about to find out whether I could be both people—Katherine the senior executive, and Katie, me.

Eventually, I came to be my whole self: *Katherine, period.* I think of my name with a period because it's a sentence unto itself. I thought, if my name was a sentence, what would it mean? Would I experience alignment, love, joy, peace, and bliss? Would I feel complete and experience self-love? Katherine was always in me. All I did was embrace that aspect of me, all aspects of me, on the outside and the way I express myself in this life time. Period.

Sincerely, Katherine. is both a multi-generational story and a series of life and leadership perspectives. I hope it serves as a source of insight, positive change, and kind and loving action for each person it touches. This book reflects on the first half of my life and the wisdom and insights I bring into this next half of my life, one that is loving, joyful, fulfilling, and impactful. I hope it represents a path, a *way home*, for each person it touches, for society and our world.

Betty Sue Flowers, author and expert on mythology and literature, shared her perspective on stories with me during a conversation we had. There are stories we tell ourselves as humans at a collective conscious level, those we tell ourselves within our family and community, and those we tell ourselves individually through our life journeys and experiences. Eight billion individual stories we are telling ourselves! Most of these are never spoken or written down; often, they are stories of hurt that have shaped our way of seeing ourselves, society, and world. They are informing our lives, often at a subconscious level. There are multitudes of stories out there that are lived and believed. And they are just stories—which means they can change and evolve. This book is simply my own story. It's my perspective, one that will continue to evolve and grow over the remainder of my lifetime.

David Bohm, a colleague of Einstein's, was one of the most significant theoretical physicists of the twentieth century. He observed that there was a widespread and growing human tendency to isolate and fragment, largely out of attributes like linear thinking and our habit of problem solving out of anxiety, fear, and survival. He saw this as a breakdown in our ability to communicate and create understanding. He believed we needed to move from fragmentation and debate (speaking solely to prove one's point) to a sharing approach centred on kindness and curiosity. Bohm envisioned a society where everyone has equal status and there is space for differing experiences, beliefs, and stories. In our conversations, we would listen. We would suspend judgement and give ourselves the opportunity to become more aware, more conscious individually and collectively, kinder, more curious and connected. This became known as a Bohm Dialogue.

Consider this book my Bohm Dialogue, one that allows us to suspend judgement of each other, to develop a deeper sense of empathy and create a shared appreciation for human uniqueness. Certainly, in my own journey I had to learn about my uniqueness. I learned to tune into my essence and soul and the things that make me unique beyond gender to know who I am at an energetic level.

I believe that three things are central to our future: our approach to science and innovation; a deep sense of knowing oneself and a connectedness with each other and nature; and a type of leadership that is driven by higher purpose and is humble, kind, curious, inclusive, and courageous.

Sincerely, Katherine. is my life story, and my life and leadership perspectives that have brought me to where I am today. I live each day with a feeling of being *home* in my heart, mind, body, and life. I am at home in my soul. I am inspired and have a deep sense of being for the next half of my life, a place where I want to be of service to others. My greatest passion is understanding and embracing human uniqueness and being part of building a world in which we unlock human potential through love, kindness, and respect.

My Journey

Visible and Invisible Dimensions of Human Uniqueness

1

Farm Fatale

---

*There will come a day, you beautiful brave soul, when
you will tell someone the truth about you, your whole tale,
and not a half truth that you have had to give the world.*

NIKITA GILL

I WATCHED FROM THE WINDOW of our farmhouse as my
parents disappeared, my father off to his factory job, my
mother to work the farm. When I could no longer see them,
I went into their bedroom. At my father's dresser, I opened a
drawer and found his drab boxer shorts and a broken alarm clock.

But I was looking for magic. So I went to my mother's
dresser. It wasn't as high, made of a light-coloured wood, with
a jewelry box and mirror on top. I opened a drawer, touched
her satin slip, examined her pretty things. I took a pair of floral
clip-on earrings out of the jewelry box and put them on and
looked in the mirror. I tried on her amber necklace, then put on
her slip and a pair of her shoes. I walked down the hallway to
the bathroom and looked in the medicine cabinet. There was a
tube of my mother's lipstick there, and I awkwardly smeared my
lips a crimson red. Back in their bedroom, I swayed in front of
the mirror and danced. I was six years old, a curious, sensitive,

adventurous, and expressive child. And I deeply wanted to feel feminine. I wanted to feel pretty.

Over time, I got more adventurous. When I was about ten years old, feeling the stirrings of adolescence, I put on my sister's undies and bra and stuffed Kleenex into the bra cups. Then I put on my boy clothes overtop and went out. I'd never left the house like this before. Now I was walking out into the world. I felt a lightness. There was a root cellar beside the old barn that we no longer used. It was damp and cool, a respite from the summer sun. The north wall had partially collapsed, the stone blocks and wood pushed inward, and the sandy soil behind it spilled into the cellar. Light came through a window on the side. I created a world in that sand, digging roads, building a farm, my own farm. I moved my toy tractor through that landscape and reveled in my secret with a feeling of completeness.

I played for a while, then felt suddenly panicked. If I was caught like this, if my secret was somehow discovered, there would be yelling. There would be anger and punishment, and my relationship with my parents would change forever. I raced into the house, took off the undergarments, and put them back into my sister's dresser drawer. I flushed the Kleenex down the toilet, destroying evidence. I was terrified of getting caught.

But I was never caught. No one ever knew my secret. No one saw my true self but me.

———————

MY DAD, WILHELM, worked as a grinder and welder at Mueller's, a factory that manufactured milk tanks and tanker trucks in St. Marys, Ontario. At the time, that part of small-town south-western Ontario was a combination of farms and manufacturing. The manufacturing is largely gone now, and the family farms have mostly been taken over by large-scale farming operations. After my parents got married, they rented a farm near the village of Anderson, the birth place of Arthur Meighen, Canada's ninth prime minster. My father's friend Jim Rankin worked with him at the factory and also ran a mink farm. My father bought six mink from Jim and started raising mink and rabbits on the rented farm. Right after I was born, they bought a farm north of Rannoch, about five kilometres from St. Marys.

I grew up on that mink farm. We had eight acres, with a gorgeous red-brick farmhouse and red hip roof barn. At the farm's peak, we had four thousand mink, which sounds like a lot, but large farms had anywhere from twenty thousand to forty thousand animals.

Mink weren't a joy for me. They are vicious, and like skunks, they can spray a foul-smelling liquid when threatened. Neither of my parents loved mink farming; like many newcomers to Canada, they were just trying to make a good life for themselves in their new country. My parents worked seven days a week. We didn't take vacations like other families did. As a child, I was embarrassed to be living on a mink farm. We had financial struggles, the work was hard, and the mink smelled horrible. The smell stayed on your clothes, in your nose.

Unlike dairy or poultry farms, where prices are protected by supply management, the price of mink is determined at auctions on an international market and set in US dollars, so both the price and exchange rate can fluctuate wildly from year to year. Mink are harvested, or pelted, in November and sold in the winter, so there is only one payday each year, and there is no guarantee of a good price. It was stressful to accumulate expenses and debt throughout the year with the simple hope that there would be a profit at the end of the year. Many years, there were losses, and the debt would be carried to the next year. In any seven-year period, my parents might have one great year, a few bad ones, and some in-between. The main markets for mink were Russia, China, and the United States. Mink is a luxury item, and when economies boom, people buy mink, but when they crash, it's one of the first things to suffer. And not all mink are created equal. There is a wide discrepancy in the quality of the pelts, so pedigree is important. My parents ran a good operation but didn't produce high volumes or pelts that brought the highest price. The precariousness of the mink market fed into the insecurities my parents had brought with them from Germany, and those insecurities came out in the form of anxiety and emotion. It was often a loud, understandably stressful household.

When I was a small child, my father still worked in the factory and my mother tended to the mink. I was left alone in a crib and would cry until I finally fell asleep. I didn't know it as a child, but this was a kind of abandonment. It came out of economic necessity, but it definitely impacted me as a young person and into adulthood. Eventually, I was able to escape the crib and move around the house freely. My curiosity was boundless. My mother called me Snoopy because I was into everything, opening every cabinet, every drawer, climbing onto the counters.

Our gender roles are learned behaviours as we get older, but as a child, I had a foot firmly in both camps, with both traditional masculine and feminine interests. I was fascinated with electronics, and when I was three years old, I took apart our radio, looking for the voice that was coming out of it. When my mother returned from the farm, I told her how disappointed I was that I hadn't found the man in the radio.

I liked anything that moved—trucks, cars, motorcycles, tractors, snowmobiles. I enjoyed building things with LEGO and wood. As I got older, I built forts outside and eventually club houses with my younger sister, Becky. My older sister, Mona (by four years), was busy with school, sports, and her friends. I was passionate at first, imagining and building my special place I could escape to, but then I would get bored with my creation and move on to something new. There was a small forest near our house that I wandered through as an explorer. At a very early age, my curiosity, knowledge seeker, and inner builder were clearly part of me.

The other side of me explored my mother's dresser, where I found beauty and pretty things. I explored her jewelry box, trying on her earrings. I had a deep desire to explore and express my inner femininity and feel pretty. I tried on her shoes, put on her slip, then examined myself in the mirror, wondering if I looked pretty. This started as early as I can remember. It became something I was drawn to and explored when I was bored and no one was around. I got more adventurous, putting on my mother's clothes, then taking her lipstick out of the medicine cabinet in the bathroom and applying it the way I'd seen my mother do. I would play with my sister's Barbie doll, making clothes out of Kleenex, sitting on the floor by our green rocking chair while my mom watched a soap opera. She would tell me there was something unique and special about me. She had no idea what I was exploring when no one was around, but she saw a very sensitive, curious, and expressive soul, one I would only come to fully accept fifty years later, two years after her passing.

———————

FARM LIFE IS, by definition, isolating, and it was even more so back then. My first real experience with socialization didn't come until I was five. The kindergarten was in South Perth

Centennial Public School, a five-minute walk from our farm. It was filled with kids from nearby farms and the hamlets in the area, most of them bussed in. There, I came to emphasize my more masculine traits and hide any feminine traits. This is where it became clear what was socially acceptable and what wasn't.

At home, my parents were under a great deal of stress, trying to make a living. Both my parents would yell when anxious or angry. My mother chased me around the house with a wooden spoon. The spoon finally split down the middle from her spanking me with it. I eventually learned to run for the stairs, where I could outrun her and she would give up and cool down. But my mother and I were very close and she nurtured me. When she came in from the farm, she would snuggle with me intently. I came to understand later that it was because she felt bad that she'd had to leave me alone in the house. Snuggling me was also her way of mourning the tragic death of her adored father during WWII and hoping that I could fill this void in her heart and life.

Eventually, I reached an age when my father could take me with him to do business and visit friends. He had an old Volkswagen truck that finally broke down completely and remained as a rusted sculpture on the farm. He bought a black Ford car to replace it. I remember driving with him to a cattle auction in it. My father bought a calf, and we put it in the back seat with a bale of straw and drove back to the farm.

The mink ate ground meat products, and my father had a few places to buy them. There was a meat clearing house called St. Marys Cold Storage, which supplied frozen meat products— mostly chicken, fish, and turkey parts—to the mink farmers. Sometimes we would go to abattoirs and pick up cow or pig parts and take them back to the farm and freeze them. I enjoyed these trips because all of the people working in these places embraced me and treated me in such a kind way. And often, my dad would stop and buy treats for us at the local gas station; Mountain Dew and pickled sausages were our favourite.

From an early age, farm kids were expected to help out on the farm. It wasn't unusual for six- and seven-year-olds to be out picking stones, milking cows, or feeding chickens.

The mink cages would gradually corrode and rust from the manure, and sometimes mink would escape. We had a German shepherd named Toby who was adept at cornering escaped mink, and it was sometimes my job to catch them and get them back into a cage. Mink have razor sharp teeth and the ability to clamp down and lock their jaws, so handling them was a challenge. You needed thick gloves and had to know how to grab them behind the neck or by the tail so you didn't get bitten. I will never forget the day one mink darted between Toby's legs and clamped down on his genitals, a horrifically painful lesson. My father was finally able to pry the mink off. But after that day, Toby killed every escaped mink. It broke my father's heart to have to put Toby to sleep, but with the help of some whiskey, he did what he had to do to protect our family's livelihood. On the surface, my dad could be loud and harsh, but he had an incredibly kind and loyal heart, and a deep love for animals. He only wanted the best for his family.

I loathed working with the mink because I hated their smell and was also allergic to them—my eyes would water and swell, and I would get headaches—though allergies were unrecognized in those days. My dad would get frustrated with me; to him, my complaints felt like excuses. In his workshop, there were posters of beautiful women wearing mink coats, and I would dream of being one of those women.

IN GRADE 1, a social dynamic began to take shape: there were the smart kids, pretty girls, mean kids, sports kids, those with learning challenges—the ones who thought and learned differently from what the "system" was designed to produce. There were bullies and the kids they bullied.

I was the kid who had my hand up all the time. The curiosity and chattiness I'd exhibited as a toddler extended into school. I wanted answers. I was very expressive, and by grade 2, my relentless curiosity and acting out became a problem. I spent a lot of time out in the hall. Eventually, the teacher, whom I adored, permanently put my desk in the corner. I felt deeply embarrassed and ostracized. Who would do such a thing to a curious and expressive child? A system designed to produce a specific kind of person, one who would help build a society and foster economic growth. A system and society that had yet to understand the unique gifts and potential inside each of us.

We were all in the same school from kindergarten to grade 8, so the roles solidified. I had a string of unflattering nicknames: Duck Shit (a play on Dudtschak), Kraut, Nazi. I was a regular target for bullies, but I wasn't alone. A girl with gorgeous curly red hair was bullied and called "Medusa." She went on to get a PhD in neuroscience. Another girl was called "Nose" and constantly bullied. She became an incredible woman and loving mother. A boy nicknamed "Femme" wasn't so lucky. I asked an old friend about him. He said he'd heard he died by suicide. For many, school is a torment, one they carry for the rest of their lives. My heart breaks for those who were bullied, for those who needed courage to face each day, and for whom each day brought pain. But today, I am repeatedly inspired by those who choose determination, courage, and kindness in spite of their hardships.

My learning challenges were evident as early as grade 2. I almost failed. My mother intervened in her direct and passionate German way, though I didn't know it at the time. Any subject that required conceptual or cognitive skills was great for me, like geography, art, the sciences. But I found math, English, and French very difficult. I could learn the even number multiplication table, but not the odd number one. I couldn't memorize formulas. Grammar was a moving target. My dyslexia was undiagnosed, as it tended to be in those days. Those with learning challenges were simply labelled "slow" or "dumb." My teacher wanted me to repeat grade 2. When my mother heard this, she went to the principal of the school and said, "You can't do this. This child is not dumb."

It wasn't until one of my children was diagnosed with dyslexia that I was able to make sense of how my mind was wired and begin to make peace with my neurodiversity, my uniqueness. As the therapist walked us through the assessment, including their challenges and incredible gifts, I couldn't help but identify personally. She observed my behaviour and saw how my mind worked, and could see I was similar to my child. She told us that dyslexia is believed to be hereditary.

So I was grateful for my mother's efforts to keep me from failing grade 2. It didn't help that I had tried to burn down the school, though. Our grade 2 teacher smoked and we knew she kept matches in the top drawer of her desk. Along with my friends Tom and Dee, I took the matches out of the drawer, and we went to the side of the school. It was a brick building, but there was wild, uncut grass that grew against the brick. We stood there and lit the matches and threw them down into the grass. We finally ran out of matches. The school remained intact. But someone told on us, and we had to serve detention

I was grateful for my
mother's efforts to keep
me from failing grade 2.
It didn't help that I had tried
to burn down the school.

———————————

outside the principal's office for several days. I was lucky that my mother was so forceful, and she could be *very* forceful, or I would have been held back.

My report cards tended to echo the same comment year after year—that if I'd only just focus more and apply myself, I'd be more successful. I have heard this same narrative repeatedly from other individuals who, like me, would discover their dyslexia and ADHD later in life. All the comments like this that I got from teachers are etched into my mind forever. Deep down, I knew I wasn't dumb. I just couldn't do things the way the conventional school system and mechanical world wanted a student to do them. And there was my little gender secret. So throughout school, I felt different, and I became increasingly determined to do it my way and prove "them" wrong.

———————

AT HOME, THERE WERE ALWAYS mink chores to do: feeding them, watering them, inoculating them, and harvesting them, which is called pelting season. The animal parts we bought to feed them had to be ground up with vitamins, minerals, and fibre. Because of my resistance to the mink, my father was constantly upset with me for not helping more.

What I liked to do was drive the tractor. My interest in anything with a motor stayed with me. I loved cutting the grass on the farm on the tractor. I felt empowered and competent. I loved the solitude and took pride in making something elegant and beautiful.

But in general, I hated the farm. I hated smelling of mink and I hated the fact that my father would get upset with me and yell. Eventually, I started to fight back. When I was thirteen and my father wanted me to help with the mink after school, I screamed, "This is not a prison camp! I'm your child!" I started crying and ran out of the house, but before I left, I could see that he was crying too. My father had survived WWII, but his trauma was something I hadn't really thought about or considered.

It remains one of the most heartbreaking moments of my childhood, and my deepest regret. My father got upset a lot, but he was a loving, loyal, hardworking man who carried an impossible burden from his past and was under tremendous stress. At that time, I knew he'd been in a prison camp, but I didn't know the details: the starvation, routinely waking up beside a corpse, sometimes a friend who'd been beaten to death in the night, a hell I wouldn't have been able to comprehend. My sense of prison camps was informed by *Hogan's Heroes*, a popular TV show with wisecracking American prisoners and dim, sympathetic German guards. But I knew I had hurt my father.

The term "intergenerational trauma" hadn't made its way yet to farm communities in southwestern Ontario in the 1980s. It wasn't something I could articulate, but I could feel it. Both of my parents had gone through hell, and so had their parents. Three of the four of them had died during the war.

Intergenerational trauma is something that is passed from trauma survivors to their descendants, through both nature and nurture. Survival genes and behaviours are passed down to the next generation, and while our genes are designed to help us survive, they have no interest in keeping us happy or creating peace. Those who survive traumatic events or live with chronic stress—and my parents experienced both—develop responses for their short-term survival. However, staying in survival mode can be detrimental to mental and physical health. Survival mode helps us deal with fear, stress, or scarcity, but if it stays activated, then we never arrive at a place of safety or security or truth.

In many ways, those generations' stress, trauma, and fear have played out in modern society as part of the collective consciousness with the belief that through education, hard work, risk, innovation, and productivity, we can create growth and prosperity for all. This "promise," built out of stress, fear, and individual desire, has not played out as intended—our planet has been severely impacted, and we have heightened levels of social and economic division, and deeply troubling levels of chronic anxiety and mental health challenges.

Owning a mink farm that carried financial stress and unending work while trying to raise three children certainly wasn't a place of safety for either of my parents. Our house contained all those fears and anxieties as well as all the hell that had happened in Germany—two generations of death, rape, and near starvation. Shouting or getting upset are two common responses to fear and pain, and our house at times echoed with what had come before.

My parents suppressed their war experiences and childhood pain to a very large extent, and carried on with determination and hard work. While I grew up with their fears and insecurities—something I'll talk about more in the next chapter—they also passed on a sense of independence at a very early age, a level of personal accountability, and courage. My parents had no conscious sense of the depth of their emotional pain, and I certainly didn't, but when I saw my father's tears, I knew something painful had been triggered. His tears were much worse than his yelling.

Not long after that fight with my father, I talked to the neighbouring farmer whose property almost surrounded ours. It was a pig farm with a lot of land. Between the mink and the pigs, I grew up in a smelly nightmare. But he had beautiful John Deere tractors and I asked him for a job. He offered me work feeding the pigs before I went to school. So at the age of thirteen, I gave up working on a stinky mink farm to work on a stinky pig farm at 6 a.m.

I am sure I broke my father's heart when I went to work for the neighbour, though at least I was working and I felt free and accomplished. The farmer eventually let me drive his tractor during harvest or plowing season. I loved it, though I did make mistakes. Lots of them. One day, I was out taking soil samples across his acreage. I drove too fast and sheared the bolts off the front-end loader while bouncing over the furrows. Another time, while spreading manure at night, I tried to take a short cut to the highway and got the tank filled with liquified pig manure stuck in a ditch. It was dark, and I thought the huge tanker had emptied on the fields, but to my surprise it was plugged and still full. The farmer had to come and pump it out to get unstuck. He had been paying me $3.75 an hour but decided to withhold seventy-five cents each hour until the end of the year. He said he'd give it to me if I didn't break anything else. It was my first experience with "carrot and stick" incentive-based compensation programs, something I would become highly experienced with during my professional career.

This farmer's two-year-old son would sometimes ride with me in the tractor. I adored him. He died in a farm accident that year, a terrible and life-altering tragedy for everyone. It was my first traumatic loss and the first funeral I ever attended. There are few things more heartbreaking than a tiny casket. My heart was broken and still hurts over the loss of this beautiful child and the pain his family endured. Most of my relatives were in Germany or had already passed away, so I didn't have any experience with death.

In all my years, I never knew my parents to attend a funeral. They would tell me they had their own way of grieving and did not want to attend. In hindsight, I realize how incredibly triggering and difficult it would have been for them, given their childhood experiences.

———————

IN ONTARIO BACK THEN, there were still thirteen grades (as opposed to the twelve in most provinces of Canada) and you could take either the five-year program that was geared toward university or a four-year program that was more vocationally oriented. I had done well in both shop class and home economics. I was good at applied studies. I knew myself well enough to go into the four-year program.

The high school was in St. Marys, five kilometres from our farm: St. Marys District Collegiate and Vocational Institute. With courses more tailored to my abilities, my marks were better in high school. I could see myself working with people, or driving or working with machines, but I couldn't see myself working with animals on a farm. I had always loved the outdoors, and I thought of becoming a forest ranger, perhaps, or a geologist or cartographer. My mind for patterns and systems was forming, and I was good at accounting, despite my early math challenges, so business was a possibility as well. These were the careers that were in my head during high school.

Because I wasn't one of the "smart kids," I hung out with the party group. I started to skip school. We would find an adult to buy us beer, and we'd drive around on the gravel roads, drinking and listening to rock music on the radio. Farm kids tend to be mechanically minded, of necessity, and often have some kind of income, either from working on their family's farm or someone else's. So there were kids at school who had their own cars. You needed a vehicle in the country—a car, truck, or motorcycle meant freedom. So we would drive the back roads in a friend's car, drinking beer, singing and talking.

The high school boys talked about music, cars, farming, girls, and sex, though not necessarily in that order. My relationship with girls was complex. In middle school, there were six or seven girls whom I asked out, even though I wasn't sure what that actually involved. I just wanted to spend time with them, to skip rope with them and be with them. But I also envied them in a way I couldn't entirely articulate.

In high school, I dated a few girls I both adored and envied. We went to movies and shared a pizza and talked, but I remained a virgin. Sitting in the back seat of someone's Dodge, drinking beer in the afternoon and listening to the guys' sexual exploits (some of them real, many of them crude fictions), I tried and had fun trying to relate, but my feelings were more multi-faceted. Partly, I was longing for companionship and love for the rest of my life already, but also, I was looking for someone I could vicariously live through.

I wished I could dance the way the girls did, dress the way they did. I wanted to express my emotions like they did. I had this complex feeling of being haunted and longing to be more like them. So I would go on dates searching for the perfect girl to experience her life as if it were my own. I was just emotionally and creatively wired more like women.

I bought myself more masculine-type clothes, like a jean jacket and lumberjack shirt, but I also loved and bought pink and soft yellow Ralph Lauren polo shirts and skinny pin-striped jeans, items that might have been viewed as feminine but at the time were simply viewed as preppy, thankfully. I thought I might be drawn to nice things because I had two sisters and a mother I was close to. It was hard to delve much deeper. Self-awareness wasn't a staple of rural life then.

It's not uncommon in the female transgender community to hear that before coming out, these women worked extra hard to gain acceptance in the male world. As assigned males at birth, many of us chose careers in the military or masculine sports to suppress our feminine or female side. We became the hardest partier, the fastest driver, the biggest risk taker. I was a regular winner of beer chugging contests. But what I longed for was complicated and not something I was going to find in small-town Ontario at that time. So I poured myself into part-time work and making money because my parents didn't have money to buy beer or clothes or albums.

Or motorcycles. Like most rural kids, I got my driver's licence on my sixteenth birthday. I had already bought a Yamaha 250cc with the money I'd saved from all that part-time work. I was queen of the road. I was free.

I loved music and bought a stereo and made my own speaker cabinets. There were songs that resonated with me, though I didn't know why. Rush's "Cinderella Man" ("this manic depressive who walks in the rain"); Boston's "A Man I'll Never Be"; Johnny Cash's "A Boy Named Sue"; Supertramp's "The Logical Song" and "Take the Long Way Home"; and Billy Joel's "Honesty." Today, I see how these and many other songs spoke to me in ways I couldn't understand back then.

My friendships began to shift in mid-high school toward being with more like-minded people, though there wasn't really anyone like me. But Ben and I became friends, and he and I would talk about having real relationships with girls. Ben had grown up on a Dutch Catholic dairy farm, and his parents were quite worldly. We still partied, drank beer or rum as we zipped along gravel roads, but we also stared at the stars and envisioned life beyond our small, cloistered world, and contemplated the universe. Ben died on November 29, 1992, at the age of twenty-six. He'd found his love and settled on his own dairy farm just north of St. Marys, and had children. He was driving with his young daughter in the car, and as he crossed the paved highway, he was broadsided by a car that was heading to a hockey tournament. Ben died instantly, but his daughter survived. This was the second traumatic loss in my life. I had felt deeply connected to Ben. He was someone I trusted implicitly, the person I could talk to. His death was a terrible tragedy for his family, for all of us. I miss Ben deeply to this day. Our souls remain connected.

WILFRID AND CARLA were friends of my parents. They were also German immigrants but lived in town. They would often come out to the farm to visit, or my parents would go into town. Carla was a hairdresser and Wilfrid worked in town in a factory that made brakes for vehicles. They didn't have any children. They were open-minded and had brought a European naturalist sensibility with them. There was a double door at the back of their garage that opened up onto a small forested area and they would sunbathe nude there. They had German nudist magazines. They were liberal, so they were interesting to me.

Whenever my father got upset with me, I would hop on my motorcycle and escape—both my father and the farm. I often rode into town to visit Wilfrid, and I would tell him about my father and start crying, and Wilfrid would listen. He was always kind. He'd give me a small glass of beer and tell me that my father was proud of me and loved me, two things I did not hear from my father. I am deeply grateful for Wilfred, for his kindness, and for bridging the gap between my father and me. It's true, it takes a village to raise a child. You never know the difference you are making as a friend, an aunt or uncle, or even a kind stranger. You could be the source of hope, belief, or inspiration that changes the path of a child.

———————

I GRADUATED FROM HIGH SCHOOL in the spring of 1984. Like many high school graduates, I didn't know what I wanted to do. But I knew what I didn't want to do, which was be a mink farmer.

2

Sins of the Father

Sometimes, it's the people who have been hurt the
most who refuse to be hardened in this world, because they
would never want to make another person feel the
same way they themselves have felt. If that isn't something
to be in awe of, I don't know what is.

BIANCA SPARACINO

ACED WITH TRAUMATIC EVENTS, human beings
develop trauma responses to help them survive and stay
safe. These adaptations can be passed on to future generations, resulting in what is known as intergenerational trauma.
The effects of the pain and suffering of one generation can echo
through the next several generations. As I've explained, the
house I grew up in contained layers and multitudes.

My maternal great-great-grandmother, Sara, grew up in a
village in East Prussia, what is now Poland. She was a beautiful
girl. I know this because my mom told me only the beautiful
girls in the village were hired to serve the aristocrats who
came to the hunting lodge. Sara became pregnant by one of
the nobles, who subsequently ignored her and her situation.
Despite the fact she was expecting, a young farmer married

her, but he never embraced the son who arrived, my great-grandfather Christoph.

As their family grew, Christoph remained apart. He wasn't allowed to eat at the table with the rest of the family. Instead, he knelt at a bench behind the large oven in the kitchen and took his meals alone. His stepfather marked the food so my great-great-grandmother couldn't feed her son when the stepfather was out working. Understandably, Christoph left home at the first opportunity. He married Elizabeth Tobinski, and they had nine children, among them my grandmother, Elizabeth, who was born June 7, 1909.

My maternal grandfather, Heinrich Schacht, was born December 20, 1909, and immediately placed in an orphanage. He grew up in post-war Germany, a country economically hobbled by the Treaty of Versailles. Food was scarce; work, scarcer. Hyperinflation had wiped out the savings of the middle class. Heinrich was tall and hungry, simply trying to survive, like so many others. He found work on a farm near my grandmother's village, where they met. They were married in the mid-1930s, with the Depression easing slightly and Hitler's Germany taking shape. My mother was born July 1, 1935, in Elbing, then part of Germany, now northern Poland.

The year my mother was born, the Nuremberg Race Laws were passed, the cornerstone of Nazi policy. Hitler had been the führer for a year at this point. The first concentration camp, Dachau, had opened two years earlier. Jews and "the politically unreliable" were already excluded from holding public office or working in the civil service. Now they were excluded from various professions and pursuing higher education. Gay men were being arrested and imprisoned (more than a hundred thousand of them between 1933 and 1945). Some were sent to concentration camps and castrated in an attempt to find a "cure" for homosexuality. The government was conducting extensive surveillance on its citizens, and people were beaten for not returning the Nazi salute. Writer Thomas Wolfe, who experienced life in Nazi Germany, said, "Here was an entire nation... infested with the contagion of an ever-present fear. It was a kind of creeping paralysis which twisted and blighted all human relations." The end of the decade would see euthanasia laws passed, resulting in the murder of between seventy thousand and ninety thousand disabled adults. Hitler's dream of a pure race— straight, white, able-bodied, and consumed by fear—was moving forward.

My grandfather Heinrich wasn't a good fit for Hitler's Germany. He played classical music on the violin and drew black and white portraits. On Sunday mornings, he would take my mother to the pub, where he had a beer with friends before coming home for the big Sunday meal at noon. My mother remembered growing up during this time as idyllic, picking wild raspberries, playing in the park in her Sunday dress, going to a cottage on the Amber Coast, playing on the beach. She was too young to sense the dark shadow Hitler had cast over the country. She wasn't alone. Canadian Prime Minister William Lyon Mackenzie King met with Hitler in 1937 and predicted history would remember Hitler as a great man. He concluded that war was not imminent. Incidentally, many years later, Canada's military and government would also go to great lengths to "purge" gay and lesbians from the system.

When my grandfather joined the police force, his family history was vetted over several generations to be sure no Jewish blood was lurking there. Hitler selected the best police officers to train as soldiers, and my grandfather was taken to a military camp where they conducted drills. On September 1, 1939, General Walther von Brauchitsch led 1.5 million troops into

Poland, my grandfather among them. Two days later, Britain and France declared war on Germany. Canada joined the Allies on September 10. The world was at war once again.

My grandfather was a peaceful man, an artist at heart, and he was disgusted by the conduct of his fellow soldiers in Poland. The invading Germans robbed, raped, and murdered the Poles. Polish cities were bombed into rubble. At this early juncture, the German army was still filled with Hitler's vision of Aryan destiny. They had taken Poland with ease, then marched into Denmark and Norway and met no resistance, reinforcing the notion of German superiority. By 1942, however, with the Americans having recently joined the fight, the tide was turning. Hitler had been advised that they needed more oil if they wanted to win the war. The plan was to invade the Caucasus and take control of Azerbaijan oil supplies.

In the spring of 1942, my grandfather was part of that effort, sent to the Russian front. The Russian campaign was initially very successful. The Germans rolled over the Russian army, driving them out of Crimea, taking Sevastopol and capturing 240,000 Russian soldiers. But the attempt to take Stalingrad was a colossal failure. For three months, the city was under siege, one of the fiercest battles of the war, fighting block by block throughout the city. The siege depleted the German forces. They were fatigued, short of supplies, and fearful of winter, that great Russian ally, which was fast approaching. Stalingrad was a humiliating defeat for the Germans: 150,000–250,000 casualties and 100,000 taken prisoner. It was the turning point in the war against Russia.

My grandfather survived the bloody Russian debacle but was shot December 4, 1943, and sent to a hospital in Riga, the capital of Latvia, where he died six days later. He was thirty-four years old. The news didn't reach his wife, my grandmother, for another week. His last words were, "Oh my God, what's going to happen to my wife and two little girls?"

My mother, Irmgard, was eight years old, and my aunt Ingrid was two, when their father died. In September 1944, Allied forces were closing in and Hitler initiated *Kinderland-verschickung*, the program to evacuate German children to safer areas. My mother was sent to a children's camp, but Ingrid was too young, and she stayed with her mother in Elbing. The camp where my mother was sent was filled with girls like her, many of them orphans.

After four months there, my mother was wakened in the middle of the night and told to collect all her belongings in the dark. The children were loaded onto hay wagons. There wasn't enough room for everyone and some of the children had to walk beside the wagons during the night. They travelled for months, moving through East Germany, staying on the back roads, sleeping in barns and abandoned castles. My mother remembered it as a grand adventure. She had little sense of the war and its horrors, but that would soon change.

By 1945, it was clear the war was lost, and the children were ordered to be placed with families. Soldiers loaded the children onto the wagons and paraded them through villages, distributing children among the villagers like care packages. My mother spent her tenth birthday with her new foster parents. But the Russians arrived shortly afterward and took the children from their new parents. My mother was sent to a Communist-run children's camp in the Russian Zone. She was sick with a throat infection and very homesick.

My grandmother was still in Elbing with Ingrid, though in the winter of 1944, they had tried to leave. There were boats leaving for Denmark and Sweden from Danzig (now Gdańsk, Poland). My grandmother bundled up Ingrid, took what they could carry in a knapsack, then put Ingrid on a sled and went to the harbor to get on a boat. She'd heard that three boats were going to arrive. Other villagers hoping to escape had heard the same thing and were already waiting by the docks.

My grandmother heard the familiar whine of airplane engines. Russian planes suddenly appeared, strafing the villagers and dropping grenades. My grandmother was knocked unconscious and woke up face down on the ground. Ingrid was lying unconscious a few feet away. She was still breathing, and my grandmother put Ingrid on the sled and towed her back to their apartment. When she took off her knapsack, she saw there was shrapnel embedded in it; it had saved her life. The noise from the guns and explosions left her deaf for a week. It was too dangerous to leave now. She felt she had to stay in Elbing, a decision she would come to regret.

When the Russians arrived, they were worse than the Germans. They dug out people who were hiding in their basements. Older men were killed or sent to labour camps. The women were repeatedly raped, even girls as young as eleven. My grandmother and Ingrid hid in their apartment, but Russian soldiers broke in. They tied Ingrid to the bed, gagged her, and raped my grandmother in front of her.

After the fighting finally stopped, the Russians took four-year-old Ingrid and placed her with a German couple. My grandmother protested but was physically torn away from her daughter and forced to march out of the village with a group of refugees. She had no idea where they were going and no idea what would happen to Ingrid. She walked for days with her fellow Germans, herded by Russian soldiers. When she was young, my grandmother had broken her ankle, and if she was on her feet too long, it would swell. On the forced march, it began to swell, finally to the point where she couldn't take another step. The Russians left her in the ditch and kept going. She started to crawl back to Elbing. It took days, but she managed and was finally reunited with Ingrid.

Poland had been heavily bombed and ravaged by two invading armies, the Germans and the Russians. The Prussia they had known was gone. It was no longer clear where home was. And my grandmother didn't know where her other daughter was. Irmgard could be anywhere. There was a very good chance she was dead.

But my mother was still in the children's camp, and efforts were being made to reunite children with relatives. A nurse asked my mother if she had any relatives in West Germany. She had an aunt Augusta in Bremerhaven. The nurse told her to write to her aunt and she would mail it to the Bremerhaven city hall. If Augusta was alive, perhaps she would get the letter. My mother also wrote a letter to her mother and mailed it to the Berlin city hall. After the war, families were scattered all over Europe, and people often didn't know who had survived or where they were, and city halls acted as message centres.

Aunt Augusta received my mother's letter and agreed to take her in, though they couldn't afford another mouth to feed; her husband had been a Nazi and no one wanted to employ him after the war. My grandmother was finally able to get in touch with Augusta and found that Irmgard was there. My mother was reunited with her family in September 1946. They'd been apart for two years.

The German state had ceased to exist; the Allied powers had sovereign authority over Germany, which had been divided into zones: American, British, French, and Russian. One quarter of the country's housing was gone, the factories had been bombed, and much of the transportation infrastructure had been destroyed. There were severe food shortages and thousands of refugees arrived daily.

My grandmother and her daughters settled in a refugee camp in the city of Wermelskirchen in West Germany. My grandmother quickly became ill and finally collapsed and was taken to the hospital. She was there for four months, leaving my eleven-year-old mother to take care of her five-year-old sister in the camp. Mom quickly became Ingrid's protector and parent, making sure they ate, that they survived.

Soup kitchens had been set up to feed the refugees, but the food was horrible—thin soup dotted with mouse droppings (and an occasional mouse) and potatoes and rutabagas that were still frozen. Each week, my mother was given food stamps for a hundred grams of meat for her and Ingrid. She knew that on the other side of the city there was a butcher who would give her double the amount of horsemeat for the stamps. So every week my mother walked there. It was winter and she didn't have winter clothes or decent shoes. She came back to the camp and cooked the horsemeat for Ingrid and herself on the communal stove in the camp. She had to watch as it cooked; if she left someone would steal it. The other kids in the camp knew their mother wasn't there, so they were sometimes bullied. On December 24, my mother and Ingrid walked across the city to the hospital to spend Christmas with their mother, sleeping on a cot in her room.

After four months, my grandmother was released from the hospital, and the three of them moved to a church in Wermelskirchen that was filled with refugees. Irmgard and Ingrid went to school with the local kids, who taunted them. "You have no clothes," they said. "You live like filthy pigs."

After four months in the refugee camp, my mother was awakened in the middle of the night and told to collect all her belongings in the dark.

———————————

Because of the acute housing shortage, property owners were required by law to rent rooms to refugees. But no one wanted refugees in their homes, and the authorities often had to intervene and force them to take them in. My grandmother, mother, and Ingrid moved in with an older couple who had a large, beautiful apartment. They didn't want three refugees in their apartment, and they were afraid of catching a disease. My mother had lice and a condition called *Krätze*, which left blisters on her hands. The kids at school called her "*Krätze* pig."

They lived in one room in the apartment, with two beds, army blankets, three chairs, and a small stove. Eventually, my grandmother was able to receive welfare, but she didn't get her husband's pension because she didn't have the necessary papers to prove her husband had been a police officer. She couldn't even prove that she'd been married. When she crossed the border from Poland, the Poles had taken her wedding ring, all her papers, and any family pictures she had. To augment the welfare money, my grandmother delivered newspapers and magazines, cleaned houses, and did laundry. She did whatever was necessary to survive.

After two years, they moved to a larger, two-room apartment. These owners didn't want them either, and the police had to intervene again. My grandmother met another refugee, who had once been a police officer. He suggested she take out an ad in the police newspaper asking if anyone knew Heinrich Schacht from Elbing. She did so, including her address, and received letters from men who knew her husband. With this proof, she was finally able to collect his pension, six years later.

The city of Wermelskirchen changed as refugees intermarried with the locals. The prejudice quietly disappeared, and it became a kinder and more generous society. But Germany was still being rebuilt.

My mother immigrated to Canada in 1960. You needed to show you had a job waiting for you in order to immigrate, and she had a friend in Canada who had found her a job on a farm. She was twenty-four. Once she arrived at the Ontario farm, my mother was essentially an indentured servant, doing farm work from 7 a.m. until dinner, then quilting in the evening. The owner threatened to ship her back to Germany if she didn't do as she said.

The farm is where my mother met my father, Wilhelm (Willi) Dudtschak. He had come to Canada in 1957 and brought his own wounds with him. His own experience with the atrocities of war.

MY FATHER WAS BORN November 12, 1929, two weeks after Black Tuesday, when the stock market crashed. My paternal grandfather, Justin Dutczak, was Ukrainian but lived in the Sudetenland (now part of the Czech Republic). He was a nice man when he was sober, but otherwise a mean drunk. He worked a small farm and cut lumber in the winter, and my father helped both before and after school from an early age. It was a hard life, and my father had no memory of either of his parents ever having fun or laughing.

In 1938, when Hitler took the Sudetenland, my paternal grandfather translated the family name to a German spelling, from Dutczak to Dudtschak. My dad was drafted into the Hitler Youth as a teenager. The organization had been around since the 1920s, but now they were sending soldiers as young as fourteen to fight what was clearly a doomed war campaign. My dad was fifteen and still in the Hitler Youth training camp when the war ended and the Russians arrived.

On May 1, 1945, the Hitler Youth were taken from their own camp and imprisoned in a Russian camp. Dad spent the next three and a half years in prison camps. Each night, the Russian guards would take a handful of German teenagers and force them to sign confessions. The guards dictated the nature of the confession, holding a gun to their heads as they wrote it out, then signed it. My dad stayed in five different camps during the course of three years. "Some camps were bad," he said, "and some camps were worse."

They moved between camps in crowded trains, fifty to a boxcar, sleeping on the floor side by side. There were no windows in the boxcars, just a hole in the floor for a toilet. Once a day, bread and water were shoved through the door. It could take a week before they got to the next camp, sitting in darkness, starving. At a camp in Tost, Poland, they numbered five thousand prisoners. When they moved four months later, only 2,500 were still alive. As many as thirty bodies a day were loaded onto hay wagons, their clothes stripped to be used by surviving prisoners. The bodies were taken to a gravel pit and dumped. A layer of lime and dirt was added, preparing for the next day's load. The vast majority died of starvation, though some were beaten to death.

Hundreds of prisoners slept in rows on the floor of a large room. At night, if the Russian guards had been drinking, they would walk along the rows and pick someone. "It could be the person next to me," my father said, "or one over, and they took him and beat him until he was gone. He wouldn't stay alive for a day." Some of the Russian guards had been in German concentration camps and now they were delivering the brutality they had experienced. More and more prisoners ended up on the hay wagon. "You knew," my father said, "that at the rate they were going, eventually it was going to be you."

To cope with this grim lottery, my father resigned himself to his own death; one day, he would be the one the Russian soldiers picked. Once he'd accepted it, the prospect of death no longer bothered him. When he shook the man beside him and found that he had died in the night, he was philosophical and matter-of-fact.

In August 1948, they closed the camps. For three and a half years, my father had lived on bread and water, reduced to skin and bones. He was eighteen, free to go home. But where was home? He didn't know where his family was, didn't know if they were still alive. The map of Europe had been redrawn. Parts of Prussia were now Poland. What had been part of Germany was now Czechoslovakia. The Russians had taken the eastern part of the country. Dad was taken to a railway station on the condition that he had an address in East Germany to go to. Someone he knew in the camp had given him an address near Brandenburg, not far from Berlin, and he gave that as his destination. He wasn't allowed into West Germany.

When he got to Brandenburg, he felt lost. He looked cadaverous and was wearing old, rotten clothes and broken shoes. All he thought about was surviving. To survive, he needed to eat. He could get a job in a factory, perhaps. Instead, he got work with a farmer, who paid him in food. He gained weight and filled out, and his strength slowly returned. Wilhelm survived— one of the lucky ones.

Wilhelm discovered that his family had gone to Halle an der Saale, in East Germany. When he got there, he found out that his mother had died two years earlier. He got an address for his father, but he had died six weeks earlier from a stomach ailment. Wilhelm's sister was in West Germany, and his brother was working on a farm near the West German border. Dad visited his brother and told him of his plan to go to West Germany and said they should go together. But his brother had a good job with a farmer, and said he was going to stay.

Wilhelm had been told to go to the railway station and wait if he wanted to get to West Germany. He waited at the station, carrying only his bag with an extra pair of shoes, some food, and a bolt of cloth in it. Others waited too. Finally, a man approached them and explained how it would work; he would guide them for a fee. My father didn't have any money, but he had brought meat and butter, which were hard to come by, and that was enough. He and seven others were led into no man's land, between the two Germanies. Their guide pointed toward West Germany, told them to walk, then disappeared. After half an hour of walking, my father didn't know if he was in West Germany or not. He hid and listened to voices, listened for clues. He had made it. Finally.

He didn't have any money, but he had that bolt of cloth, enough to make a suit. In those days, if you found something that felt like it had value, you kept it. He went from store to store trying to sell it, but no one was interested. Finally, a merchant bought it, and my father used the money to buy a train ticket. It took him only partway to Remscheid, where his sister lived, so he needed another train, and he was able to sneak on one, but was caught by the conductor. My father explained he was a refugee from East Germany on his way to his sister. The conductor was kind enough to let him stay on the train until he reached his destination.

Dad found a job in a steel factory in Remscheid and worked there for ten years. With the money he saved, he bought a motorcycle and toured Europe, going through Bavaria, over the Alps, through Austria, and into Italy, a country he loved for its weather, countryside, and food. Wilhelm reveled in the freedom that had been unimaginable only a few years earlier.

His brother was still in East Germany, but he told him how to escape and sent him money. His brother finally arrived and Dad got him a job in the factory where he worked for the next thirty years, until he retired.

Wilhelm came to Canada in 1957, when he was twenty-eight. His sister, Christa, and her husband, Paul, had already immigrated to Ontario. Christa had known Irmgard in Germany, and it was she who got my mom the job at the Ontario farm. My parents met on that farm and were married in 1961.

My sister Mona was born the following year. I was next, born March 9, 1966. "I don't want him," my sister said. "I want a pretty little girl like me." Little did she know.

3

The Determined Imposter

God changes caterpillars into butterflies,
sand into pearls & coal into diamonds using
TIME & PRESSURE. He's working on u too.

RICK WARREN

AFTER GRADUATING HIGH SCHOOL, I applied to several colleges in various cities: Sault Ste. Marie, North Bay, Peterborough, Kitchener, and Stratford. I applied for business, cartography, geology, and forest ranger programs. I was all over the map. In the end, I decided to enroll in a business program at Conestoga College. Conestoga was situated in Kitchener but had a satellite campus in nearby Stratford that offered a two-year business diploma.

Who could predict that I would go on to become a CEO with a degree from such a small college? And yet I had a business mind even then.

My math and logic were simple: I had chosen the four-year high school diploma instead of doing five years, and I would do a two-year business program rather than four-year. I was saving three years. And in those three saved years, I could make money. I liked nice things, and you needed money to buy them. My older sister, Mona, whom I looked up to, was living in Calgary and doing well working in accounting for an energy company. I was determined not to live the life of my parents; I would find the perfect job and perfect partner and have the perfect family. And business had an aura of prestige attached to it, so it might be a way to achieve all of that.

Stratford was only a thirty-minute drive from the farm. But as home to the internationally acclaimed Stratford Shakespeare Festival (now just Stratford Festival), it was culturally worlds away, and the campus was next door. I would look out the window and wonder about the world of art and culture that existed inside its walls. Next door, Hamlet and Romeo and Juliet and Othello were all repeating their tragic lives onstage each night, but I missed it—I went to the theatre only once. I was busy partying and working part-time jobs to make money. Looking back, I realize that by then I had already suppressed my feminine and creative interests, and that might be partly why I didn't make the theatre a priority. When I was a kid in public school, I was in choir and did pottery; I loved to sketch and paint. And I suppressed all of those creative interests to just party and make money so I could go out and buy nice things. To some extent, I was dealing with my anxiety by not being present, by working and spending money. Those were the early days of my becoming a workaholic.

Initially, I lived in the student nursing dorm because the campus for the business program did not have a dormitory. I felt relieved to be away from the farm, happy to have the independence, if emotionally conflicted around the mostly female nursing students.

But after four months, I ran out of money and had to move back home and commute every day. I got a part-time job working for my friend Ben's parents on their farm, milking cows and harvesting corn. But this still didn't give me enough money to pay for school, so I got another part-time job in a car parts factory, pressing out galvanized fuel lines and running the reclaim machine, which took discarded pieces of fuel line piping and recycled them for another use. Despite the two jobs, I still needed to borrow money. I knew my parents didn't have any, so I borrowed $1,000 from a bank. It seemed like a lot of money then, and I was already worried about how to repay it. Joe, the owner of the local gas station and Ford dealership, offered to co-sign my bank loan. He got to know me when I would stop for gas on my way to school. He saw potential in me that I did not see in myself.

In my first year, there was an economic downturn, the beginning of the hollowing out of the auto industry in southern Ontario, and people at the factory were being laid off. I couldn't afford to be laid off, so I went to the plant manager in tears, and said, "I'll do anything. Please don't lay me off. I need this job to get through college." I couldn't afford to take on any more debt. To my surprise, the manager kept me on amid all the layoffs, and that job paid for much of my college. I learned that sometimes it pays to put aside your pride and tell people what you need. People can be surprisingly empathetic.

I wasn't comfortable at school or home, but increasingly, I was running into individuals who saw something in me and wanted to help me in life. In the summers, I worked for the St. Marys Landscaping company. I was attracted to the machines and being outdoors, but I was also drawn by the fact that my sister Mona had worked there, and two other women—sisters Joyce and Joanne—also worked there. I idolized Mona and was following in her footsteps. I worked in the lawn care division. It was a dream job for me. I drove massive lawnmowers through town, queen of my kingdom, empowered and free. Out working on large residences and park and factory lands, I was in my own private world, alone with my thoughts.

In my second year of college, another landscaping company offered me a job that paid more. They wanted me to run their lawn care division. I needed the money and took the job, but I missed working for St. Marys Landscaping, specifically working with Joyce and Joanne, who were the kind of girls I wanted to be with. They were funny, kind, pretty, hard-working, and confident in a man's world... the kind of girl I wanted to be.

Years later, when travelling back to St. Marys with my four children to see family, I would drive them crazy, pointing out all the beautiful properties I used to take care of. "Oh, I used to cut that lawn," I would say, repeatedly, and they would scream, "Stop, please stop!"

My marks continued to improve, and in my second year, I became president of the student association. This brought opportunities to plan more parties and social activities, but it also brought my first real leadership responsibility: handling complaints and advocating for disadvantaged students.

I graduated from college in the spring of 1986. My plan was to work for an insurance company. I could move to Winnipeg and work for Great-West Life or to London and work for London Life. Kitchener had Manulife. Many of the large insurance companies were in the area. But one day, by chance, I reconnected with one of my dearest childhood friends, Rob, whom I hadn't seen in several years, and this changed the trajectory of my life.

His girlfriend's father was the branch manager at a bank in St. Marys. For a poor farm kid, the branch manager of the town bank was a god. In my view, this was the top rung of the local business world. Most farms and businesses flowed through him. I remember standing in his living room, and he was in his recliner. "Katie," he asked, "what are you going to do now

For a poor farm kid,
the branch manager of the
town bank was a god.

―――――――――――

that you're graduating college?" I told him I'd applied to a few insurance companies. He said, "Why not apply to the bank?" I could be a loans officer or a branch administration officer, he told me. They had training programs for people coming out of college and university. I hadn't considered this—working for a bank wasn't on my radar at all.

I wasn't interested in loans, but I was drawn to working with people. Deep down, I had a curiosity about people, about humanity. Ultimately, I wanted to lead, so I applied for the branch administration officer training program and was surprised when I got an interview. The interview was to take place at the bank's offices on King Street, in the heart of the country's financial district in downtown Toronto.

I had never been to Toronto. It was only two hours away, but it was like a mythic kingdom to me. I drove down in my parents' 1972 green two-door Plymouth Fury. I had asked directions ahead of time from one of the women who was going to interview me. Unfortunately, she gave me the wrong directions, and in those pre–Google Maps days, there was no immediate way to solve this problem. I crawled through rush-hour traffic, going in the wrong direction. Even after I found parking, I knew I was going to be late, which only made me more anxious.

Jogging along Bay Street, I looked up at the towers in awe and fear. Here I was, a poor farm kid, heading for the nerve centre of the country's biggest bank. Everyone seemed to be in expensive clothes and cars, and looked like they knew what they were doing. I had struggled to learn in school. I had a four-year high school diploma, not five. I had two years of college, not a four-year university degree. I had grown up on a mink farm, on another planet. I was an imposter, but I wanted to fit in so badly.

I sat across from two women who looked calm and competent. I was an hour late, flushed and apologetic. Not a great first impression.

"You're awfully young," they said. "Why should we hire you?"

"I believe in working hard for your goals while you are young," I said, "so you can benefit from them in the future."

This seemed to make an impression. But by the end of the interview, I was still nervous. I'd been late, and I didn't have the qualifications. Surely, everyone else they were interviewing had more impressive resumés. Just before leaving, I looked my interviewers in the eye and said, "I'd better hear from you. I want this job." They were surprised by my boldness. So was I.

But I didn't expect to hear from them. A month went by, and I didn't get a call. I assumed that was the end of my banking career. Then one day in July, I was offered a job as a trainee in Woodstock, Ontario. I didn't know it at the time, but this was a path I would stay on for the next thirty-five years.

———

THE 1980S WERE the Wild West of capitalism: deregulation, junk bonds, privatization. Canadian Prime Minister Brian Mulroney, US president Ronald Reagan, and British Prime Minister Margaret Thatcher were all arguing for free markets, for unfettered capitalism. In 1987, the movie *Wall Street* came out, giving us the catchphrase "Greed is good." None of this made much of an impression on me, but there was another movie about the financial world that came out the same year. *The Secret of My Success*, starring Michael J. Fox, spoke to me.

Fox stars as Brantley Foster, a college grad from Kansas who moves to New York to work in finance. I identified with Brantley, another imposter (literally in his case—he takes on a fictitious persona in the film) who makes it big in the big city. I couldn't see a place for myself among the people I'd seen walking down Bay Street, with their university educations and MBAs (I assumed), people who understood money and the world much better than I did, but Brantley showed me another way in. He wasn't sophisticated, but he won people over with his ability to communicate and his hard work. I also identified with his love interest, played by Helen Slater. She both took my breath away and filled me with envy. While Brantley's career journey spoke to me, I was drawn to Helen on a deeper, much more complicated level.

A few years later, the movie *Pretty Woman*, with Vivian, played by Julia Roberts, would come out. Oh, how I wanted to laugh and shop like Vivian. Oh, how I wanted that brown and white polka-dot dress. It would take thirty years before I could have my own.

I MET ROSEMARY in August 1986. By this time, I had moved to Woodstock, Ontario, and was working as a trainee at the bank branch there. A mutual friend who worked in road construction introduced us. He knew her from work; Rosemary was an inspector on road construction sites. We all met at a bar, Gables, in the beach town Grand Bend, on Lake Huron. I was blown away by her beauty and energy, how vibrant she was, and how confident she was working in a male-dominated profession. Once again, I put myself out there, and it worked. Within a year, we were engaged.

The Woodstock job lasted about nine months. Rosemary and I were married in August 1988, two years after we'd met. I was determined to have a successful career and knew that could mean moving around a lot, and I was afraid that if Rosemary and I weren't married, I'd lose her. We needed that commitment to move around together from town to town, city to city.

There are different ways to get ahead in the banking world. One is to start in a big city or at the head office and move up, eventually ending up on the top floor. But I still felt like an imposter and knew I needed to be flexible, mobile, and opportunistic to get ahead. I was prepared to go anywhere, to move to cities and towns that others would never consider. After Woodstock, I was transferred to Cambridge, where I was an assistant manager. It was a step up, though I still felt out of place. It was a very traditional male environment, and I had trouble relating, though at the time it was hard to say why.

In spite of that, I loved the clients. A Mennonite farm family used the bank for their more complex services, and I often helped them out. They had a large sod farm, and eventually they offered me a job running their lawn care division. I was twenty-one, and part of me was still trying to prove something to my father, and I thought, *My god, I could own my own business*. I'd worked in landscaping before. So I left the bank.

Unfortunately, it wasn't a good time for the lawn care business. There was a severe drought that year and everyone's lawn was dying. I was working with chemicals and my farm headaches came back. It wasn't long before I missed the bank. I missed the people. I definitely missed the air conditioning! So I begged the bank for my job back. I was hired back a week before our wedding and appointed assistant branch manager in Blenheim, Ontario, near Windsor, my third town in less than three years. Within six months, I was offered another promotion, this time to take care of business clients in Chatham. Rosemary and I bought a house in the nearby village of Glencoe. I still felt like an imposter, but I was having some success.

My success with the business arm led to the offer of assistant branch manager there too. The branch had problems, and

I was the keen, eager Brantley who was going to fix it all. Except I didn't fix it—the challenges proved to be more complex than I could imagine. The bank finally sent in Human Resources to review the branch, and I was criticized for not communicating as well as I could have. I had felt communication was one of my strengths! I was also chastised for skipping across the floor— it was a (too) feminine expression of joy. Men don't skip, and bankers certainly don't skip. I was given a final written warning, the corporate equivalent of death row. I felt judged and rejected. HR subjected me to an intense interrogation, after which I was a zombie for weeks. My fragile sense of self had been shattered. It was the darkest point in my career.

To compensate, I worked harder and longer than ever. I came home late from work every night. I was buried in my career. A new senior leadership team was sent in by the bank. The new area manager and branch manager saw potential in me and encouraged me to learn and move on, and that gave me hope, but I still wanted a change, a clean slate.

Rosemary felt that she, too, should be able to pursue her career. I empathized with her and encouraged her to go back to school. Like me, she had gone to college, but she wanted to get her university degree in civil engineering. In part because I was living vicariously through her, I could feel how unfulfilled she was. Rosemary applied to the engineering program at Lakehead University in Thunder Bay and was accepted. I was able to get a transfer there. Not many people wanted to transfer to Thunder Bay because it was so far north, but I did. I loved nature and the wilderness, and you didn't have to get far out of Thunder Bay to experience it. So, a fresh start for both Rosemary and me.

To my surprise, both the Thunder Bay area manager and deputy there embraced me immediately. "Don't you know what's in my file?" I asked, referring to the final written warning. They said, "We don't care what's in your file. We can see who you are as a person. We can see how genuine you are. We want you on our team." After my devastating experience, it was wonderfully affirming that they saw potential in me.

I flourished in Thunder Bay, and within eighteen months, I was offered another promotion, this time as deputy area manager in Timmins. It meant another move, and Rosemary had another year left for her engineering degree. But she believed in and encouraged me, and we decided to take the promotion. So for most of the next year, we commuted back and forth between those two northern communities, over seven hundred kilometres apart. I remember going through Rosemary's drawers during this period. I wasn't dressing up in women's clothes, but I looked at her things and wished that I was her, that I was a woman.

Eighteen months later, I was offered another promotion, this time in Cornwall. Rosemary got a transfer to Kingston, so we moved to Morrisburg, a tiny town between Kingston and Cornwall.

IN SPITE OF my challenging school years and the skipping experience in Chatham, I was developing a reputation for learning quickly, building things, and fixing complex problems. I was known for being determined, friendly, outgoing. Once again, in spite of my imposter syndrome, more and more mentors and sponsors saw something in me that I couldn't.

Years after Chatham, a dear colleague from Human Resources called me one day and said, "Katie, today is the day. Today, the final written warning is being removed from your file and destroyed." He wanted to tell me personally, which was uncommon. I was moved to tears as the buried anxiety of that difficult time began to lift.

From Cornwall, my next job was in Burlington, the provincial headquarters, working closely with my mentor and regional executive. It wasn't Bay Street, but it felt like the big time. I was moving all over Ontario, but what I really wanted at this point was to be in the head office in Toronto. As luck would have it, I was given a special project to work on in Toronto, in the King Street building where I'd been interviewed years earlier. The project was to build operational models—technology and processes that could be rolled out across the country. I was working with brilliant people, some with PhDs, and consultants from McKinsey, the global management and consulting company, and although I'd had several promotions over a short time, I still couldn't shake that feeling of being a fraud. I feared they would finally figure out I wasn't that smart, that I had other secrets. I didn't know I had a gender secret at the time, but I had traits that made me feel very different.

I decided that, like Rosemary, I should go back to school. What better way to banish the imposter inside me? The MBA program at the Ivey Business School at Western University gave credit for work experience. It was the top business program in Canada. I applied and was accepted. It was a rigorous program, but my experience did have certain advantages. The program used case studies to illustrate business problems and solutions, and my last several years had basically been one case study after another. I wasn't good with theory, but faced with complex real-world problems, I could find solutions. I'd found them before.

For the first several years of our marriage, Rosemary and I had been consumed by our careers, and we were simply too busy for a family. Initially, it was a conscious decision not to have children. But then we started trying, and nothing happened. Several years went by, and finally we both got tested. There appeared to be nothing physically wrong with either of us. The doctor just told us to slow down, to remove some of the anxiety and stress in our lives. We hadn't realized how consumed with education and work we'd been. It was the boiling frog syndrome; it just kept getting hotter by degrees and we didn't notice.

Then, Rosemary did get pregnant. At the time, I was trying to finish my MBA while continuing to work full time at the bank. I was exhausted all the time. I empathized with her as she endured the challenges of pregnancy, but I wasn't much actual help. I was still focused on building a better life than my parents had, focused on proving the bullies and teachers wrong. Focused on proving to myself that I was worthy.

And then our first daughter arrived.

She was born the day I graduated with my MBA. We finally had a family. And everything changed. There is nothing like the birth of a child to show you the beauty and fragility of life. I fell head-over-heels in love. Suddenly, family came first rather than work, and I felt a deep obligation to provide for my family, to give them the resources I didn't have growing up.

But work pressures remained intense. I was doing strategy work at the bank offices downtown. Some senior people were in as early as 5:30 a.m., and I felt pressure to be at work by 7:30 a.m. It was a way of getting approval, of being seen and accepted. I was still so deeply worried about being judged or criticized. Early mornings became long days, and evenings could stretch into client dinners. It was the cultural norm at the time for corporations. Executives prided themselves on working iron-man hours.

Thankfully, my boss, an incredible executive and a single mother, also became my role model for both work and family life. She made it her priority to drop her two daughters off

There is nothing
like the birth of a child
to show you the beauty
and fragility of life. I fell
head-over-heels in love.

——————————

at school and have dinner with them each night. She maintained that she would not arrive in the office before 8:30 a.m. and would leave by 6 p.m. each day. She was bold, informing her senior leaders that she couldn't attend 7:30 a.m. meetings. Through her example, Rosemary and I alternated. I would take care of our daughter in the mornings before the sitter arrived, and work later. Rosemary would go to work early and arrive home early.

It takes bold, courageous leaders to change culture and organizations, and I was blessed to have a pioneer as a boss. Little did I know how often I would have to draw on her boldness and conviction over the years to come.

It is incredibly difficult for any employee who is carrying inordinate amounts of fear, shame, or guilt to fully express themselves and be confident in their work. Like so many others, I felt I had to make up for it by working long hours. The MBA had helped my confidence, but the imposter still lurked just beneath the surface. At one time, there were problems with the project I was working on, and I felt I was failing. I asked my boss, "Am I doing an okay job? Should I be looking for another job?" "You're doing an amazing job," she assured me. It was hard for me to have any real perspective. I still carried those schoolyard insults. I was still the child who would have failed grade 2 if her mother hadn't intervened. My desk was still in the corner.

Three months later, I was offered an executive posting leading Eastern Ontario for the bank. I would be overseeing Ottawa, a bilingual city, and I didn't speak French. This felt like a leap of faith on the part of the bank. But the important thing was that they had faith in me. Rosemary found a great job as a civil engineer in an engineering firm in Ottawa. We were off on yet another adventure.

Our first child was almost two, and in the summer of 2000, Rosemary became pregnant with our beautiful twins. They were born in February 2001. We stayed in Ottawa for four years. Our fourth child was born in Ottawa too. Four children in four years. With both parents working. It was chaos—controlled and beautiful, but chaos nevertheless.

Given the ever-changing dynamic and sometimes difficult lives we had been living, we started defining our periods of change and challenge as "just another Dudtschak Adventure." This became our family slogan. Everyone in the family would finish each other's sentences: "Oh, we've got this, it's just another Dudtschak Adventure." Little did we know how many Dudtschak Adventures we would face together in the years to come.

By this time, we had fallen in love with the Ocado family, whose three sisters and aunt would care for our family in four cities over the next twenty years. We would also purchase a family cottage outside Dorset, Ontario, which would become our special family place and anchor home as we now began to move around Canada as a large family of six.

I was very close with Rosemary's sisters and her brother, George. George and I went off on weekend retreats put on by the Landmark Forum, which advertised a transformative learning experience and offered ways of increasing empowerment and fulfillment in life. He was curious about the meaning of life and I desperately wanted to make sense of myself and why I had certain feelings. George was someone with whom I could have deeply personal conversations, much like my friend Ben and I did years earlier.

One weekend at the cottage, George and I talked about what we would do if one of our children were gay. George could be an intense, masculine guy, but he had a kind heart and was in tears when he said he would be faced with a choice: "I could love them for who they are, or I could reject them, be estranged from them and reconcile on my deathbed. I think I'd want to love them for who they are."

I was deeply touched by that. I had often wondered if I was gay and remembered punching my pillow as a teenager thinking, *I must be gay!* Did I know I was gay at the time? Did I know I had a gender secret? No. Something was haunting me, though I couldn't put a name to it. My empathy with women had increased with the birth of our first child. Something stirred, some feminine and female part of me that hadn't been allowed to fully come to the surface. I had deep feelings and questions, but no answers.

And some part of me still overcompensated on the masculine side. I was a weekend warrior, partying hard. A thrill seeker. I drove my snowmobile and boats fast. I skydived. I was intense in my work, and some of that spilled into our home life. As a parent, I was more authoritarian and less patient than I would have expected or wanted. When I yelled, I could hear echoes of my parents yelling at me. These patterns repeat themselves. I was trying to teach my kids life lessons, and in hindsight, I know my father was probably trying to do the same thing. It was just his version.

One of the lessons I tried to impart to my kids was that in life, all you own is your name. Despite my success, I still felt I could lose my job tomorrow. And if I did, what would I have? I was trying to teach that in the end, you are left with your own character, your own soul. Ironically, it was a lesson I had failed to fully understand and embrace myself. What I had wasn't my name but what others thought of me. The true self-worth, self-respect, and self-knowing didn't arrive until years later.

When I started out after leaving home, I was driven by the desires to have a life that was better than my parents' lives had been and not let anyone stand in the way of my abilities. I wanted to find a good job and a wonderful wife, to have children and financial security. My ideal was a throwback to the 1950s, and I had achieved all of that. Then why wasn't I feeling complete? Everything around me was perfect—at least by my initial goals and standards on the outside. The thing that wasn't perfect, or aligned, or complete, was me. I still couldn't articulate why. I remained a mystery to myself.

This would be the next and most critical step on my journey. It would also be the most frightening and challenging phase of my life.

4

This Time, My Transformation

People may call what happens at midlife "a crisis," but it's not. It's an unraveling—a time when you feel a desperate pull to live the life you want to live... The unraveling is a time when you are challenged by the universe to let go of who you think you are supposed to be and to embrace who you are.

BRENÉ BROWN

I WAS FIFTY YEARS OLD when I finally began to zero in on my truth. It began in the fall of 2016, when I drove my eldest daughter to Queen's University, in Kingston. In the hallway of the dorm she was moving into, there was a poster of someone assigned male at birth wearing a silk blouse and pearls. Beneath the image, it read, "Embrace gender variance." The image resonated with me. Momentarily stunned, I stared at that poster and thought, *Could the world become so open that I could be me?*

I still didn't know what "me" actually was, but I was inching closer. For years, I had been hovering over that question. It was like scratching an itch that wouldn't go away. I would google "emotionally sensitive men" or "fashion fetish," and what came back was usually focused on disorders or fetishes that were offensive and hurtful and didn't fit. I knew I didn't have a disorder, but I couldn't pinpoint what I was feeling and experiencing. This may sound naive, that a fifty-year-old senior executive living in Toronto wouldn't be able to figure this out. But I was raised in an isolated community, and in a way, I had remained sheltered. For years, my world was work—it and my version of the "perfect life" consumed me. And for much of my career, I was living in smaller centres, not the kind of places where you run into gender diverse people. I was living in a sort of bubble, with guardrails to keep me on track and fences to keep me protected.

A few months after dropping off our daughter at Queen's University, I was at my barbershop, waiting for a haircut. There was a *National Geographic* sitting on a table with the cover line "Gender Revolution." I picked it up and read about young men and women whose brains and hearts were wired differently from the sex they were assigned at birth. This concept was completely foreign to me. When I got home, I went online and ordered that issue of *National Geographic,* and when it arrived, I gave it to Rosemary. "You never know," I said. "In case one of the kids is gay." *Or your spouse.*

Then, in May 2017, my mother died. We were exceptionally close. She was the one human being whom I felt had a window into my soul. She understood me, even though I didn't entirely understand myself. She used to tell me that I was special, that I had a gift for relating to people. I felt seen by her in a way that no one else had ever seen me. So I was shattered by her death. She hadn't had an easy life. It had begun in the horror of war, and the years on the farm were hard, but she was very comfortable in later life, content and at peace. And she had a peaceful death. I was devastated and I missed her terribly.

The week after her death, I was going through her house with my sisters, Mona and Becky, preparing it for sale. We were going through her things to see what we wanted to keep. We were in her bedroom, and my sisters looked at our mom's jewelry box. They both said they didn't want it. Then they looked at me and said, "Katie, you should have it."

They didn't know the meaning it had for me, but they remembered that I had bought it for her for Christmas years earlier. I opened the dark wooden box and immediately began sobbing. Partly, it was because I was missing my mother, but a large part of it was the fact that I knew every piece of jewelry in the box. I had a vivid flashback of my six-year-old self trying on her clip-on earrings, her necklace. I remembered going through her drawers as a child, imagining that I would find a million dollars there. I could see how other families had more money and I instinctively knew we were struggling. I had this idea that my parents secretly had this huge cache of money they were keeping from us kids, and I was convinced that I would find this million dollars and all our problems would be solved. These memories swept over me and I sat on the bed in my mother's empty house and cried uncontrollably.

———————

IN JULY 2017, one of my children confided in me that they were questioning whether they may be gay or bisexual. I told them I had wondered if I was gay when I was their age. I would come home from school, overwhelmed with this thought that I was somehow different. I would go to bed and punch my pillow in frustration, thinking that something was wrong with me. That I must be gay. But it didn't feel quite right. I understood their confusion.

For me, the reality turned out to be much more complicated. Over the course of several months, I was moving closer to my truth. The epiphany came on August 25, 2017, at 12:35 p.m.

I was having lunch with a dear colleague. We were at a sushi restaurant not far from the bank offices. He was gay and a corporate champion for the 2SLGBTQ+ community. I asked him how he knew he was gay. It was simple, he said: when other boys were looking at photographs of women modelling underwear in the Sears catalogue, he was looking at boys in underwear.

I asked him what being transgender meant, and he patiently explained the difference between gender identity and gender expression, between binary and non-binary. I asked about Caitlyn Jenner; how was it possible to go from Olympic men's champion to Caitlyn? He explained that Caitlyn had always been Caitlyn on the inside. She poured herself into sports and her career with that intensity to prove to others, and to herself, that she was masculine enough, that she could be a man. It was a way to suppress her feelings and true gender, to stifle aspects of her essence.

And I thought, *Oh my goodness, that sounds like me.* I didn't have much else in common with Caitlyn, but this struck a nerve. And she was attracted to women, just as I was.

"Gender is who you go to sleep as," my colleague told me. "Sexual orientation is who you go to sleep with."

That lunch conversation was the dam breaking. For decades, I had been keeping a finger in the dam, patching leaks when they sprang up. But now, the dam broke with epic force and flooded my brain. I left that restaurant a changed person forever.

I went home that evening and googled Caitlyn Jenner again. This time, I read and understood differently. And that took me to other links about transgender, and now I was reading all this information with a level of focus and clarity that had been missing before.

The dam broke with epic
force and flooded my brain.
I came out of the restaurant
a changed person forever.

———————————————

I was in shock. I literally became a zombie. Over the next few days, Rosemary could tell I was distant and lost. She asked what was wrong.

"Nothing," I said.

All I wanted to do was tell her what I was thinking and what I felt was likely true. But I was afraid of losing her, of losing my family. I felt like I had betrayed her.

Ten days later, in our bedroom, Rosemary again asked me what was wrong. This time I summoned the courage to say, "I think I'm transgender."

"What's that?"

"I think I'm wired female on the inside." I broke down in tears.

For the next two months, I didn't do much other than talk to her about these feelings and cry. In November, I started looking for a psychologist and a gender therapist. I needed the psychologist to help me emotionally, and I needed someone with experience in gender issues to guide me.

During the day, I remained a dedicated, high-functioning senior executive, but outside of work, I was consumed by questions and fear. My work kept me sane and productive and sustained a level of self-worth that kept me going; it had become intuitive, and I could rely on my thirty years of experience. Ironically, the results my colleagues and I delivered through this period were record breaking, a real lesson in the power of experience and intuition, keeping things clear and simple, and an incredible team.

My difficult work became my time away from the bank, which was consumed by distress, exhaustion, and trying to prove or disprove my gender truth. I focused on my mental health and emotional well-being.

I met with a psychologist who advertised herself as an expert in gender. After almost six months of regular meetings,

I asked, "When are you going to diagnose me? When are you going to tell me if I'm transgender or not?"

"I had you diagnosed during our second meeting," she said.

"You diagnosed me *the second time we met*?" I couldn't believe it. At that point, I was still building trust with her, trying to make sense of my life. I was still trying to find a comfort level, whether I could be fully open or not, and she had diagnosed me on the second meeting?

She took out the *Diagnostic and Statistical Manual of Mental Disorders* (DSM) and set it on the table. "Read it for yourself," she said.

The DSM, currently in its fifth edition, is essentially a psychiatric encyclopedia that catalogues every known disorder. It can be a useful diagnostic tool, but it also creates boxes that people are slotted into. It has been criticized by some psychiatrists as essentially a laundry list that you can check off, a substitute for clinical expertise. And of course, it attaches the word "disorder" to everything. I was appalled. I didn't feel like I had a disorder. I just felt I was wired differently.

"I fundamentally disagree with you," I said.

She offered to set me up with a group of cross-dressing men who met once a month. But this felt wrong to me and reductionist of how I was feeling. What I desperately wanted was to either prove or disprove that I was a woman on the inside. Part of me wanted it to be true. I just wanted to be me. And part of me wanted to disprove it so I would not have to face my truth and hurt my family. But I wasn't going to find that here and we parted ways.

I reached out to a highly renowned therapist who specializes in gender dysphoria. Over two months, we met regularly. He was both a researcher and a therapist, and his questions were extensive, objective, and without emotion. I told him that I related more to women at an emotional level, and I told him about dressing up in my mother's and sister's clothes when I was a child.

"And you never got caught?"

"No. Never."

"Everyone gets caught."

At a subconscious level, he explained, they want to get caught because they want someone else to see them as they see themselves. But in my case, the consequences would have been too terrifying.

In May 2018, my therapist told me I was in the 97th percentile for anxiety, which is the most severe, and I had "severe gender dysphoria." Gender dysphoria is the disconnect between your inner being and your lived experience physically. In my case, they were extremely disconnected.

My anxiety had spiked almost immediately after the lunch in August 2017 when my colleague and I had discussed Caitlyn Jenner. Because I now had an answer to a question I had been wondering about for fifty years. I was going to bed crying almost every night, worried that I would hurt my children and Rosemary, and about whether the world could handle my truth.

Along with my visits to my therapist, I was consuming every book and article on the transgender experience that I could get my hands on. I read more than fifty books in nine months. I was looking for answers, for hope, in women who had been embraced by their family, friends, and colleagues, and in women like me in the corporate world. By the end of May, I was certain I was wired female. I was already beginning to express parts of my suppressed femininity with a little makeup, some clothing, my body language. Each step felt completely natural and part of me. It was subtle, but it was public. I asked myself, if I were as the woman I wanted to be, what would I eat? What would I do with my hair? By summer, I had lost twenty pounds.

I was eating healthier. My hair was getting longer. I was experimenting with makeup. It was a way to bridge the gap between my authentic self and how the world saw me. The world saw me as male, but it was starting to see a different version.

To cope, I needed to embrace parts of my true self and incorporate them into my daily life. My dysphoria was so intense, I could not begin to comprehend living a double life. The thought of being anything but my true self created unbearable anxiety for me. While I have deep respect for those who travelled similar roads and were able to lead a double life, I could not. I would not have survived.

THE TRANSGENDER or gender diverse brain is wired differently. When a baby is delivered, their gender is declared based on their genitals. An easy call. This is your assigned sex at birth. But psychiatrists have only recently been asking, Where is the gender? What if it's not in the genitals? As an embryo forms, the genitalia form into male or female, but the brain and body can go in different directions. It is known that the physical body and genitalia form in a different trimester from the brain, further increasing the chances for differences in development. The masculine and feminine brains are structurally different, and a baby born with a penis may have a structurally more female brain.

It isn't only structure; the female brain functions differently. There are studies where researchers used MRIs to view images of the brain as people performed different tasks. The brain activity of transgender people often resembled that of the gender they identified with, not the one they were assigned at birth. Some MRIs showed gender diverse brains that were somewhere between male and female.

Our traditional view of gender has been binary. But there is a body of research and experience that shows that gender exists on a spectrum, and we now have new categories along that spectrum: non-binary, genderfluid, genderqueer. This explained a lot for me. Both gender and sexual orientation exist on a spectrum. Western socialization and social norms have deeply reinforced a binary view of gender and sexual norms, but many Indigenous cultures have long recognized gender as being on a spectrum. Some celebrate this form of human uniqueness as a gift, one that allows a Two-Spirit person to relate to two worlds or be their true multi-faceted self with the gifts that come with it.

My brain and heart had gone in one direction, my body another. Essentially, I had been at war with myself my entire life. Maybe this was where my ability to relate to people came from, the ability to instinctively understand both sides of an issue. But now, what I wanted, what I needed, was to be able to relate to myself.

I confided in my sisters, Mona and Becky, and two friends, Lee Anne and Mike. Eventually, I told a few more friends. All of them would become critical to my survival and the well-being of my family over the months and years to come. I was blessed to have a very supportive network in place.

In July, I saw an endocrinologist for hormone treatment. Hormone treatment for gender affirmation involves suppressing the sex hormones determined by the person's assigned sex at birth while maintaining sex hormone levels within the normal range for the person's affirmed and true gender.

I started with the suppression of testosterone. It was hoped that suppressing testosterone alone would provide emotional relief. It didn't. My anxiety and stress got worse. Your body and mind needs hormones to remain balanced, and both my body and mind were increasingly unbalanced. The period between the summer of 2018 and February 2019, when I was suppressing only testosterone and not yet receiving estrogen, would prove to be the most difficult of my life.

I FINALLY KNEW my gender truth. I could no longer run or hide.

What I didn't know was what came with that truth. I believed that I was going to hurt Rosemary and our children, that my company wasn't ready for me, that the world wasn't ready for me. I was slowly embracing the real me. On the one hand, that felt amazing. But at times, I was deeply depressed. In August and September 2018, I had my first thoughts of ending my life.

I had worked hard to create the "perfect" life. If I ended it now, it would be the end of a perfect life. If I made it look like an accident, my children wouldn't carry the burden of my suicide. They would mourn their parent, the person they had known all their lives. I felt that Rosemary deserved to be free to build a new life. She could do that if I were gone. And I would be remembered for the life I had created. The alternative of facing life and my journey ahead seemed so hard.

I had done the work with therapists to prove my gender truth and gender dysphoria, but the coping mechanisms weren't working. I had intense fear of rejection and abandonment, and even a fear of being homeless—all of that was through the roof. Ending my life seemed like a perfect solution, yet my dear friend Lee Anne called me on my perfect plan. Lee Anne and her husband, Mike, were close family friends. Mike and I met during MBA school. Lee Anne was a psychiatric nurse working with homeless people on the streets of Hamilton.

Suicidal ideation is a frightening thing. More than half of 2SLGBTQ+ youth have thoughts of suicide and they are 3.5 times more likely to attempt suicide than the general population. For transgender people, the rate is 5.9 times more likely. I was middle-aged, had access to health care, and was surrounded by an amazing network of friends and family. My heart breaks to think of the millions of 2SLGBTQ+ people who don't have access to the love and support they deserve, to mental health care—those who don't have a network and the resources to seek help, who are alone with their confusion on their journey. I want to tell them they aren't alone. That our stories can become their stories. That there is hope.

In the darkest moments of my depression, I actually felt like I was sinking into a deep pit, and as I fell deeper and deeper, I could hear my children talking and other people carrying on with their lives. And at the same time, my logical mind was telling me to snap out of it. But I couldn't. It was a very dark, very frightening place to be.

Since childhood, when I was often left on my own, my biggest fear was of being abandoned. The feeling was always there, under the surface, which was part of why I had four children and why I surrounded myself with so many friends. I had built a proper life as a corporate executive so I wouldn't be rejected and also to prove that I could build a better life than my parents. The fear of losing everything was always very real to me.

I was lucky that the darkness passed. But it would return sometimes in intense spikes.

———————

IN MARCH 2018, after I shared my truth with my friends Nancy and Bob at our annual life-planning retreat, they both were so loving and kind. We cried together for a long time. They insisted we have conference calls every Sunday morning to help me on my journey and protect my well-being.

In August 2018, after my Sunday call with them, I wrote a letter of intention to myself titled "Embracing Me." If I wasn't ready to show my true self to the world, I could at least declare it to myself. The opening quote was from Jan Morris, a famous author (and part of the first team to climb Everest), who affirmed her gender in 1972 and became the most public gender-affirming person of her time.

In her 1974 memoir, *Conundrum,* she wrote:

> To me gender is not physical at all, but is altogether insub-stantial. It is soul, perhaps, it is talent, it is taste, it is environment, it is how one feels, it is light and shade, it is inner music, it is a spring in one's step or an exchange of glances, it is more truly life and love than any combination of genitals, ovaries, and hormones. It is the essentialness of oneself, the psyche, the fragment of unity. Male and female are sex, masculine and feminine are gender, and though the conceptions overlap, they are far from synonymous.

In my letter of intention, I wrote:

> For much of my life I have had feelings of not fitting in or being different. Feelings I was like a girl, feelings of relating to women more than men, feelings of a want and desire to be more like women I admire. Feelings of wondering if I was gay, of wishing I was born a girl.

I have a medical condition called gender dysphoria, where I feel and see the world through a feminine lens or sense of self, but was born in a male body. I am what we describe in today's world as transgender, where in my heart and mind my identity is female but my body and how the world sees me is male.

Research suggests hereditary and hormonal influences on the timing of the fetus's body and brain development are drivers of this condition. This mismatch is the foundation of gender dysphoria, where the misalignment of mind and body triggers periods of longing, frustration, anxiety and depression, and unhappiness with elements of the body, mannerisms, and clothing. The way to deal with this mis-alignment is to bring the physical and hormonal self into alignment with one's sense of self and identity.

Over the years, I have experienced shame and self-loathing, hoping it will go away. I dealt with denial and fears of loss and rejection. The intensity of this feeling grew stronger as I got older. It has been like poking a hole in a dam where the water rushes out faster and faster, having been held back for many years. Or like popping a champagne bottle after shak-ing it. There is no plugging the dam or re-corking the bottle.

I also wrote a manifesto for myself, essentially taking stock of the situation and formulating a plan.

I now understand and accept that I have a severe level of gender dysphoria, and that this has been part of me my entire life. It has not been straightforward or easy given the accepted worldview of gender as binary, and has generated feelings of shame, guilt, anxiety and depression. That said, I have no regrets. I have incredible kids who are open and talented and will make a difference in this world, a strong, amazingly talented partner, loving and accepting friends, and an incredible career where I have found ways to make a difference and be increasingly impactful.

Self-acceptance has not come easy, given the fears and risks transition presents for me, my family, and friends. The steps toward transitioning are taken to resolve deep feelings of anxiety, depression, and dysphoria, but in turn create new feelings of anxiety. This should be liberating, yet it doesn't feel liberating. I accept and embrace the fact that this is my reality. I am confronting this at a time in history when this condition is much more understood and accepted, and I live in a country and work for a company that are open-minded, and have a group of friends and family that are incredibly loving, open-minded, and supportive.

I take little steps every day to learn, discover, and work toward my alignment. I choose to take and make this journey with self-love, and love and gratitude for others. I am doing this thoughtfully and humbly, with a desire to do this better than it has ever been done before. I am embracing and owning it, enjoying the journey and the blessings along the way.

When I wrote this, I believed it at a logical and intellectual level, and I hoped some higher power would help me. But I was still struggling with shame and self-hate, and I was deeply afraid that my company wasn't ready for the real me. And it wasn't just the company. While my immediate friends and family had been amazingly supportive, I was very worried about how old friends might react.

This was on my mind when I went back home for a wedding. My childhood friend Ben's daughter was getting married. She was the one who had survived the car accident that had killed Ben. I wanted to go to her wedding, to help her celebrate

I had to deal with
the fear that the world
wouldn't accept, let alone
embrace, me.

———————————

and see her family, a family that had meant so much to me. But I was mortified at the thought of going home. It would resurface buried memories, many of them bad. I was on edge the whole time I was there. It was a Catholic wedding, and I feared that they wouldn't be able to accept me.

Of course, the wedding was beautiful and I connected with some old friends. Yet all I could think about were my childhood experiences with bullying, and the beautiful boy so cruelly nicknamed "Femme," whom I understand died by suicide. And I thought about how some religions do not embrace people like me. When my spouse and I drove back to Toronto the next morning, I cried uncontrollably the whole way. All I could think about was how the real me would be rejected. Rosemary could see my distress but didn't know what to do. She was beside herself.

As we drove down the highway, my thoughts of suicide became a plan. I would have an accident. A freak accident.

Thankfully, I never followed through. Weeks later, I told my friend Lee Anne, who is a psychiatric nurse, that if an accident happened and my life ended, it would have been a full and perfect life. She looked at me and said she would send me articles on how suicide creates multi-generational trauma. And at that moment, it suddenly hit me. My plan would not work. Lee Anne and Mike would figure out it wasn't an accident. Rosemary would figure it out, and possibly the kids would as well. There was enough multi-generational trauma in the family already. It was at this point that I said to myself, *I can't die by suicide. I just can't do it.*

But it meant I had to find a way to deal with the feelings of shame and self-hate that I'd had for decades. And I had to deal with the fear that the world wouldn't accept— let alone embrace—me. I felt like a caged animal.

More than a year had gone by since the lunch that changed my life. And except for my work, I had spent most of that time alone. I had distanced myself from colleagues, family, and friends. But I couldn't continue this way. It was time to tell.

On December 19, Rosemary and I told the children. The kids ranged in age from fifteen to twenty then. The six of us were sitting on our bed with our dog, Shilo. (Shilo was named after a village in Manitoba. Through our many Dudtschak Adventures, Shilo was our deeply trusted companion and loving friend.)

Rosemary began the conversation gently, saying that they'd probably noticed something was going on with me. She went on to explain that I was wired female on the inside and that I might have to do something about it, that I might have to embrace my true self. Then I elaborated on what Rosemary said, telling them how I had been feeling, how living with the conflict had brought me to the point of feeling like a caged animal. We had been coached to keep it short. Rosemary's version might have been two minutes. Mine wasn't any longer. We paused to let them respond.

My youngest daughter said, "What pronouns would you like to use?"

One of the twins, who loves dirt bikes and snowmobiles, said, "Will you still want to ride snowmobiles with me?"

Of course!

Our oldest daughter, said, "You better come out to the bank before you retire, because you're going to rock the world."

And then we all looked at our other child, a deep, quiet soul. They were the one with the greatest opportunity to pick up on the clues. A few months earlier, the two of us had been driving up to the cottage. I had put together a playlist with songs like "Dance Like Nobody is Watching" and "Be True to Yourself." And they'd picked up my phone and saw on Spotify that I'd done a search of transgender and 2SLGBTQ+ songs. They put their hand on my shoulder while I was driving, and said, "Is there something you want to tell me?" There wasn't, not then. But here we all were, on the bed, and they were the last to weigh in.

"What do you think?"

They just shrugged their shoulders. "So what?" was their response.

The reaction of my children was beautiful, and it spoke to the open-mindedness of young people today. A world away from my own generation, when I was growing up.

But within a few days, I was once more worried I would hurt my children and they would reject me. I wondered if they were thinking their parents would separate, they'd lose their home, I would lose my job, and their lives would change drastically. My anxiety was contagious, and that Christmas, our home became a pressure cooker. To deal with that pressure, I quit drinking; alcohol is a depressant, something I really didn't need then. I did not touch alcohol for two years after that. It was very hard because society is always offering it and putting us in social situations where it's there, but I stopped cold turkey. I was so afraid of falling into the pit of depression, feeling utter despair and just listening to life carrying on around me.

I spent New Year's alone, at home, watching a movie and eating popcorn, pondering the next steps, both looking forward to and dreading them.

THE NEXT STEP was to start full hormone therapy. In early February, I began taking estrogen. Within a week, I felt tremendous relief. I was full of joy and experienced the first real period of calm and peace I'd had in eighteen months.

Estrogen treatments slowly make the body more feminine, resulting in breast growth, decreased body and facial hair, a softening of the skin, loss of muscle mass, and redistribution of body fat.

The treatments are designed to reduce gender dysphoria and improve emotional well-being through calming the mind. Physical changes evolve over a few years. But my relief was almost immediate. Part of it may have been psychological—I was finally beginning a process of hormonally moving along the spectrum, my body catching up with my heart and mind.

The next step was to tell my colleagues at work. Banking is an inherently conservative world, understandably, since part of our job is to conserve and protect people's money and the economic stability of society. I was terrified of being judged and rejected. I thought I might lose my job. I was leading almost 30 percent of the company's employees—more than twenty-five thousand people. I had led successful transformations in my corporate life. Now I had to lead the biggest transformation of all.

I talked to a dear friend, Doug Elliot, a lawyer who had helped pass gay marriage laws in Canada. A recipient of Canada's highest honour, the Order of Canada, he told me to first come out to the most senior person possible. He assured me that all would be okay. That it would be very difficult to not accept one of the most senior executives in the country. So I decided to come out to the CEO of the bank. I had always felt we had a good relationship. I went into his office on February 13, 2019, and cried for an hour as I told him my secret. That evening in a text message, I thanked him for being so kind and caring in our meeting.

Later I received a reply: "I can't believe what you have been carrying and I can't believe your courage. I've got a lot to learn. The company is with you." I was deeply moved by his response.

The next day, I came out to my immediate boss and the head of Human Resources. They were both wonderful. The head of HR empathized with me on my journey, and said, "I am your protector." The relief I felt was overwhelming.

In early March, I flew to New York to meet with Monica Prata, who runs Gender Expression Care, a company that helps people express their true gender. I had found her on the internet more than a year earlier. Monica had a background working as a makeup artist for MAC, and at Nordstrom in women's fashion. She had once felt marginalized herself and had great empathy for the 2SLGBTQ+ community. At Nordstrom, when certain men came in just before closing and awkwardly inquired about makeup or clothes for "their girlfriends" or "wives," she recognized what was really going on. She helped them, then finally started her own business, recognizing there was a need for this service. I had looked at the photos of the women she had worked with and read their hopeful stories about how they were able to live as their authentic selves. But I wasn't ready then. My dysphoria was so bad that I knew if I saw and liked my true self, there would be no going back, so I had painfully delayed seeing her. But I was ready now. Monica would guide me through a feminizing process that would allow me to see what my authentic self would look like.

When I arrived in New York, the first thing we did was go to her apartment and talk for three hours about my gender and journey. She believed more in me than I did at that point. After our conversation, she knew that I would need to embrace my gender all the way and all the time to feel complete. I felt that she understood me in a way no one ever had before.

We went to Neiman Marcus, Saks, and Nordstrom to see what worked. Monica would bring thirty items to me in the dressing room as I slowly discovered my style. Iranian designer

Elie Tahari's clothing was perfect for me. We picked out hair that worked for me, then had it styled. We went to the MAC store and Monica did my makeup. In her apartment, I put on a dress, some jewelry, the hair. She explained what she was doing with the makeup. A brilliant makeup artist can disguise bone structure. The whole process took two hours. Then she said, "Okay, turn around and look in the mirror."

It was the most euphoric moment of my life.

The first words out of my mouth were, "Oh my god, I can see my daughter." I thought I looked like an older version of her.

My second reaction was, "Oh my god, I love me."

What I saw was *me*, for the first time. It was an awakening. We did a photo shoot. I still carry one of the photos on my phone. And we picked my chosen name. The best practice is to keep your initials, so you don't have to change your signature. So I was stuck with a K name. I toyed with either Karen or Katherine but had trouble picking one.

"Just pick what feels right," Monica said.

"I think it's Katherine slash Katie."

"There you go."

Katherine felt strong and graceful, and Katie was lighter, more playful. I liked the combination. It felt right. It felt like home.

I had no idea what my name would mean or represent. It was a choice by feeling, sound, and intuition. For years, I had proclaimed to my children, "All you have is your name," your word, your character. For so long, I felt this was a contract with the outside world, to fit in. Little did I know it was my word, my integrity with myself, my soul.

There is a "Katherine" in each of us. Katherine is a feminine name originating from Greece, meaning "pure" or "clear." Throughout history, the name has been associated with purity, honesty, discipline, wisdom, and enlightenment. My spiritual name is Ahna, meaning "pure," "favour," and "grace." It is a reminder to be true to oneself. Katie is a name that reminds us to embrace our lighter, playful, loving, innocent, and creative self. These attributes, all of them, would speak to me deeply, to my soul, over the years to come.

Michelangelo said, "The sculpture is already complete within the marble block, before I start my work. It is already there, I just chisel away the superfluous material." Another of his famous quotes also resonates with me: "I saw the angel in the marble and carved until I set him free." Little did I know that my life, my choices, would eventually chisel away the unneeded pieces of marble to reveal my essence, my truth, so I could embrace all I am and would become as human being, as a *woman*. As Katherine.

———————

MY NEW WORLD was beginning. My new world was opening up. Monica and I went for lunch, with me as Katherine, my authentic self. It was exhilarating. I felt I was being seen for who I am in the world for the first time. Monica coached me on how much food I should put on my fork, tried to correct my (still not great) posture, gave me tips on how to use my voice.

That night, I decided I would go to a Broadway play on my own, as me, as Katherine. I decided on *Wicked*, a reinterpretation of *The Wizard of Oz* story, this time told from the perspective of the witches. Both Oz stories deal with the theme of transformation, so the choice was perfect for me. I was wearing heels, a great dress. My mannerisms weren't fully evolved yet, and my voice hadn't yet adjusted.

I left Monica's apartment and walked to the subway station. I'd never taken the subway in New York before. It was a test: I was in the world alone for the first time as me. The subway is New York laid bare—crowded, raucous, occasionally dangerous. This was part of the fabric of the city. I was worried about being stared at and judged, or worse. But the ride was uneventful. I emerged from the subway at Times Square and walked to the theatre where *Wicked* was playing. I was a little late, and the curtain was rising as I shuffled along to the middle of the row, wondering again if I was being stared at and judged.

The *Wizard of Oz* features creatures seeking some kind of transformation. The Tin Man wants a heart, the Cowardly Lion seeks courage, the Scarecrow needs a brain, and Dorothy wants only to find her way home. But her search, ultimately, is for something that is already inside her (as it was for her friends). As Glinda the Good said to Dorothy, "You've always had the power, my dear, you just had to learn it for yourself."

All of this resonated with me on the deepest level possible, sitting in the comforting darkness of the theatre as my authentic self, my own transformation beginning. I had always had the power within me, and now I was starting to feel it.

5

A New World

To transform and elevate, you may be required to go it alone. You will have people and things removed from you so that you can search within and find YOUR POWER. Trust that during this period you're being directed towards peace, healing and growth.

ASH ALVES

ON MY WAY HOME from New York, I wrote down a critical path for my coming out and transformation. I still had to address my colleagues at the bank, a daunting and, at times, crippling thought. A dear HR colleague volunteered to delay her planned retirement to support me in my coming out. "Katherine, this is your journey," she said. "Everything needs to feel right for you."

There were already things that didn't feel right. Someone had sent information to my family about conversion therapy—the idea that, with therapy, I could live life as a man. I was both hurt and appalled. And there were a few friends who objected to my coming out, on religious and "moral" grounds. They felt I could simply continue to suppress my authentic self, that I could put my finger back in the dam. But at this point there was no dam; the floodwaters had washed it away. Carl Jung said, "Who looks outside, dreams; who looks inside, awakes." I had already awakened.

Before I came out to the bank, I wanted Rosemary and my closest friends to see me. To see Katherine. They deserved to meet the real me first, and I felt it was critical to my peace of mind as well as theirs. I arranged for Rosemary, Nancy and her husband Rob, and Lee Anne and Mike to fly to New York in early May 2019 and stay at a hotel at Union Square.

Monica spent the afternoon getting me ready. Then Rosemary came to Monica's to meet me for the first time. We were both incredibly nervous. Rosemary was warm and kind and gave me earrings and a necklace as a gift. The two of us went to a nearby Japanese restaurant and sat side by side. Near the end of the evening, only Rosemary and I and two men sitting at a nearby table were left. They kept making small talk, engaging us in conversation, flirting. Rosemary was in shock, while I thought it was funny and felt validated as a woman.

The following evening, we planned a dinner for us and our friends at a nearby restaurant. We booked a private room that was filled with spring flowers. I prepared a speech to introduce them all to Katie: "I want to take this opportunity to introduce you to Katherine, or Katie for short. While I know Katie's been here for as long as I can remember, you may not think you know her ... Katie is a bit complicated. She loves to love..."

It was a beautiful, very emotional experience. But the next day, I had to fly back to Canada to my old life. The following weeks would be the most emotionally challenging of my professional career. Being transparent at work was something I wanted. I knew enough as a business leader that if you show vulnerability and authenticity, you could earn the right to have people's trust. And hope that they continue to believe in you.

But that's just it. I was going to have to trust them not to reject me, and I was going to have to trust and believe in myself, while putting myself, Katherine, out there in a way that I hadn't before.

My first step was to write a letter to organize my thoughts. My Human Resources colleagues knew that it was my story to tell, that it had to be told the way I wanted to tell it, with vulnerability and honesty. They were amazing at saying, "It's your coming out. We'll be guided by you." So I proposed we go to the board of directors first, the top executives next, and then my direct reports. And then on June 17, 2019, we could tell all employees.

The plan was to record a video in which I explained my transformation to the bank's more than eighty thousand employees. It was the CEO's idea to do the video—I need to give him credit for this. He volunteered to be in it and wanted to do the right thing and be by my side. He was so supportive. In late April, I went to Grip Films in Toronto's film district and recorded the video. It was in a large warehouse space, with a producer and a dozen technicians. I was nervous at first, but the producer quickly calmed me. I was there for five hours as we went through my truth.

The video mirrors my letter. The man who recorded the video and interviewed me reminded me of the older man in the movie *On Golden Pond*. He was calm, kind, and loving. He had a grayish beard and masculine voice, and he used my letter as a guide to interview me. One of my dreams is to have an Oprah-like show on which I interview people about their human stories of hope and transformation. People open up to me about their hurt, struggles, and journeys... it's humbling and something I cherish deeply. But this man really had that gift. I trusted him completely.

Later, the CEO of the bank and my boss shot their own input, which was edited into the final video. With the five hours of recording they created a six-minute video of me and my story.

"Dear colleagues," I said, reading my letter in the video, "I am writing to you today to share something very personal and ask for your care, compassion, and support. I am also writing to you to explain changes you have seen in me and will see in the months to come. As long as I can remember, I have felt different, assigned male at birth, but feeling and being female on the inside. I've been thinking about this letter and how I'd explain myself to friends and colleagues for years.

"The process of figuring out who you are and how you're wired is the most challenging, difficult, and emotional experience I could ever have imagined. When something is so deeply ingrained and a part of you, it's next to impossible to put it on the shelf.

"You can't. It consumes you. I am proud and comfortable to come out as being transgender. I can't shut this off. I accept it as part of me and part of being human. On one hand, you have answers to who you are and you're finally able to take steps to expressing it and owning it. Yet at the same time, you create disruption for the people you love the most. What I worry about is a loss of trust, the loss of credibility as a senior leader with the people I lead and work with.

"Over the coming months these changes will continue and I will begin living life as my authentic self. When I return to work this fall, and [to] my role of executive vice-president, I will change my name to Katherine, or Katie, and will use 'she' and 'her' pronouns.

"The process of creating alignment between your inner sense of self and your physical and social self is a journey. It takes time and it takes exploration. The picture I'm going to share with you is . . . me."

At this point, I held up the photo that Monica had taken of me. The camera zoomed in for a close-up. There I was, smiling, radiant, a glimpse of my true self.

"I'm happy to introduce you to Katherine, or Katie," I said. "For the first time in my life, I had a chance to see me. I had feelings of me, but to see me in a way that I would want to express me was the most profound experience of my life.

"I know at the core of my being that my experience, my soul, my values, aren't changing, but it will take time for people to see that. My ask is that you don't avoid me, that you feel free to ask questions. I am happy to talk about my journey and struggles.

"You make our company and Canada the kind of place where my family and I feel safe and supported. I'm not only encouraged, I'm humbled and I'm inspired. It gives us a lot of hope for the world of tomorrow."

The person in the video doesn't completely look like me as I am now—a woman living in my essence, in my truth. Before my coming out, I wore some mascara, and a couple of people at the company had tuned into that. I wore a little foundation to clean up my complexion. I had lost weight. My hair was longer. My mannerisms were beginning to be more expressive. My hands would move more. I was no longer able to fully hide my feminine, female attributes.

In late May, we told the board of directors and then the most senior executives and peers, just as I had proposed. On Sunday, June 2, in a quiet executive meeting room at the Fairmont Royal York hotel, we told my leadership team. I had never organized a Sunday meeting before, and they came from across the country—Halifax, Montreal, Ottawa, Waterloo, Winnipeg, Calgary, Vancouver, and Toronto. Once they were all seated, I left the room.

My boss said, "We've got something important to share with you about Katie, and we'd like to let Katie tell you herself."

Then they played the video. After, they experienced a brief diversity training course. I came back into the room, and I cried uncontrollably. "Surprise!!" I finally said.

I apologized for bringing everyone in on a Sunday and was met with hugs and understanding. I told them I had wanted them all to have a chance to view the video and process it before it went out to all employees. I wanted them to be ready to help lead people through this transformation.

On June 17, 2019, the video went out to more than eighty thousand employees. The response I received was overwhelming. Within days of it being shown, I received dozens of emails, which quickly grew to hundreds, and eventually thousands.

"I don't know you. I probably never will… I watched your video this morning. I was literally reduced to a puddle at my desk."

"From you, I saw so much courage. You are, in so many ways, what I wish I could be. Fearless, even though there's a lot at stake, concerned about the impact of something—a decision like this—because you could lose so much, yet still foregoing. I am so proud of you."

"I am so proud of you. I don't know you at all, and I cannot even imagine how much courage it took for you to sit in front of that camera."

"I saw your video, and was both humbled and inspired by your courage."

"I looked into your eyes so hard in hopes that you could somehow feel my energy and love from one soul to another. I wished so hard that I was able to reach thru the screen and just touch you, hug you... Katie is beautiful and it fills my soul to know her."

A colleague and member of the Black community, whom I'll call James, shared with me his experience watching the video. He checked his email and started to watch the video and was almost immediately in tears. His wife asked him what was wrong. "You'll never believe this," he said. Together they watched the video, crying together. I asked him why it was so moving for him. James said, "Katie, as Black people, we watched a white senior executive of one of the largest banks in the world show vulnerability and come out to the world. We were in awe, and had this profound feeling of hope that perhaps the corporate world and broader world could become so kind that every human being could be embraced for who they are, and achieve their potential."

Other employees played it for their families. And families came together. One woman told me a story of her daughter having come out to them recently as gay. And they watched my video and cried together, and they looked at their daughter and said, "You're going to be just fine."

It wasn't my goal to give people hope; it was a wonderful side effect. We were a long way from the time I was reprimanded for skipping.

I had come out publicly in my senior executive role because I wanted to keep my job. I chose to be vulnerable in order to increase the likelihood that colleagues would feel my authenticity and give me the chance to prove myself to them. I didn't want to give up my career, and I was terrified that I could lose my ability to provide for my family. The public nature of the video, and the fact that it included my boss and the bank's CEO, was an endorsement that sent a message out to the bank's tens of thousands of employees.

We were a long
way from the time I was
reprimanded for skipping.

_____

The video came out on a Monday. I was in the office because I didn't want to be home by myself, but I didn't schedule anything. I wanted to give everyone some time to absorb my news. But on Thursday, four days after the video, I was scheduled to appear onstage at a town hall meeting in front of five hundred bank leaders.

I sat there at the back of the conference hall, waiting to be introduced, extremely nervous, with hundreds of eyes on me from the moment I entered the room. The flood of emails had been uplifting, but this was a live audience. I didn't know what to expect. I was introduced by one of my close senior colleagues, and before he was finished with the introduction, there was a spontaneous standing ovation. The audience sat at tables of eight and I had to weave my way through them to get to the stage. People moved to step in front of me, wanting to hug me on my way to the stage. The walk to the stage took forever. The ovation wouldn't stop. It went on and on. It was a huge collective embrace, an incredible, deeply emotional endorsement beyond anything I could have ever imagined.

I was still presenting as my old self, but we spent almost half the time I was onstage talking about my journey. It was the elephant in the room. I told everyone about how I had spent my life wondering about my identity, and about how liberating it was to finally be able to embrace my true self and be free of a deep secret. Then we focused on business as usual for the rest of the meeting.

Ten days later, a very dear friend and colleague arranged to host a reception for me at her house. She invited a handful of close colleagues and spouses, and this time, I was going to present as Katie. Monica flew up from New York to help me with my new self. It was a wonderfully affirming experience to appear as Katie with people who knew me. Also, I didn't want my colleagues worrying about me or what I would be like. I wanted them feeling confident and secure as they supported their employees in the weeks to come.

But I still had to do the heavy lifting. It was euphoric presenting as Katie, but now my physical self needed to catch up. Three days after the reception, I was on a plane to Buenos Aires. I had done my hormones and was ready for surgery. This would be a big journey.

I had never been to Argentina and didn't speak Spanish, and at that time I had no real experience travelling around the world alone. There are dozens of places where you can have feminization or harmonization surgeries performed. I chose Buenos Aires because it was affordable and, like California, it was highly reputable. My surgeon was Marcelo Di Maggio, who specialized in tracheal shaving and facial feminization surgeries. Tracheal shaving is essentially getting rid of, or at least reducing, the Adam's apple. This isn't simply a cosmetic procedure. While all humans have the Adam's apple, it is an identifying masculine feature and is highly visible. To be rid of it is empowering.

Facial feminization surgery deals with the inherent differences between male and female bone structure—the jaw, the shape of the brow, the cheekbones. I was in Argentina to have three surgeries in five weeks. Two required a general anesthesia and significant recovery times. Dr. Marcelo Di Maggio's clinic, MDM, had other surgeons on staff, each with their own specialty—everything from rhinoplasty to body sculpting. I was fifty years old ,and through puberty and testosterone, my body had developed in a masculine way: the nose got bigger, the brow line was larger and protruding. The essential bone structure needed to be altered, softened.

I was afraid of being alone and lonely, healing both physically and emotionally, in a foreign country where I didn't speak the language. Rosemary couldn't accompany me because she needed to be there for our children, three of whom were getting ready to go to university for the first time that fall. So I assembled a rotating team to help me while I was there. For the first week, George, my brother-in-law, was with me. He agreed to join me within seconds of receiving my email. During our many years together, George and I had a lot of wild experiences. This time, we had our nails done; George chose proud pink toes. So sweet and so affirming. The second week, my sister Mona came. We drank coffee and relived our family life together. It was great to have that family support. The third week, Monica came from New York, and the fourth week, my friend Mike was there. Mike and I spent endless hours solving the challenges of the world, just like we always had.

The first surgery was eight hours under a general anesthetic. Ten days later, I had another surgery, which lasted nine hours, also under a general anesthetic. The healing process was challenging, and I missed my children deeply, crying most mornings. I was unaccustomed to being away from them. I used my time to check into the office, reading and returning the countless emails I received after my coming out, or what is better put as my *letting in*—letting the world into my secret and true self. I was profoundly moved by the kindness and embrace I was receiving from people, and even more moved by the stories of their own struggles and vulnerability they shared.

Buenos Aires was charming. I had rented a lovely condo and we went out to wonderful restaurants. I had to use makeup to conceal the bruises after surgery, but the food was incredible, and it was a joy to be out as my authentic self.

The third surgery was for hair transplants and needed only a local anesthetic, but it was eight hours. It took a lot to heal. Luckily, I am a quick healer and painkillers were a huge help. After more than twenty-four hours of surgery and five weeks, I had healed enough to fly home.

I worked from home for the rest of the summer and officially changed my name to Katherine.

ON SEPTEMBER 6, right after Labour Day, I returned to the office as Katherine, as Katie. It had been a prolonged coming-out period, from first telling my bosses in February, coming out to the whole company in June, and finally returning to the office in September. I had worked remotely during the summer so I could continue to add value, have purpose, and remain connected during a very stressful personal time of transformation.

This isn't the norm. Often, transgender people lead a double life, where they are their authentic selves in private but essentially in disguise at work. When you're ready to come out, you tell the boss and HR on Friday, then take a week off and return to work as your authentic self. So, to extend my coming out over a period of months was a bit abnormal. But I did it that way for several reasons. When I went to New York to meet with Monica in March 2019, when I still hadn't fully expressed my gender, I had a gut feeling that if I saw myself in the mirror as my true self, if I took that step, I wouldn't be able to lead a double life. Once I crossed that line, I wouldn't be able to go back. Emotionally, it would be difficult to retreat to what was essentially a disguise. I knew my gender dysphoria and my feminine tendencies were so strong that I couldn't go back.

Another reason I extended my coming out over several months was more strategic. The corporate world is typically conservative, and I knew in my heart that if I was going to be accepted, even embraced, I needed to give my colleagues time to learn about gender and adjust to the idea of who Katherine really is. If employees received training on gender and inclusivity, about deadnaming, using the right pronouns, and so on, then I would experience fewer feelings of rejection or judgement. I also knew that in my emotionally vulnerable state, deadnaming, being addressed with the wrong pronouns, or more overt forms of judgement could severely impact my mental health. I had led corporate transformations, and I used that vulnerability, knowledge, and insight in my own transformation. I understood how to care for and take people through challenging times.

But I still had to face the world. You can retreat or you can put yourself out there. I decided on the latter. Between October and December, I travelled across the country doing town hall meetings. I had to take care of business and make sure everyone was focused on our strategy and work as I'd always done, but I also wanted everyone to see me, to experience me as Katie, to see that I was still a highly capable human being and senior executive. Those town halls were incredibly validating for me.

The annual top performer convention was held on a cruise ship, with a thousand employees on board. I was overjoyed at the acceptance; employees lined up for selfies and to talk and show their kindness. I was the host of the town hall meeting with hundreds of employees and my boss and the CEO watching. I was nervous. It was impossible not to think that I would walk onstage and be judged. And if I failed as Katie, the consequences could be harsh—it could affect my career.

In my mind, the voice of my dear friend and coach, Ralph, played loudly: "Katie, I don't give a shit what gender you are. All I care about is that six months after your coming out, you are even more talented and impactful than ever!"

After the presentation, my boss told me he was blown away. As Katie, I was a more effective and compassionate leader, no longer distracted by my dysphoria. But there was another step to getting there. A big one.

My gender-affirming surgery had been postponed for a variety of reasons. To have the surgery done, you need to apply for government support, and there was a backlog. You also need a doctor's endorsement (or in my case, one from two doctors) stating that you are truly suffering from gender dysphoria, that you are mature enough to make the decision, that it's a conscious decision, and that it is in your best interest. The surgery clinic itself had a backlog as well. And then COVID-19 backed things up even more. So I had to wait, watching as weeks turned to months.

Eighteen months went by before I could go to Montreal to have the operation done by Dr. Pierre Brassard at GrS Montréal, which does more than one thousand surgeries a year. Dr. Brassard is internationally renowned and served as a visiting professor at the Mayo Clinic to teach gender-affirming surgery. So I felt I was in good hands.

Oddly, the gender-affirming surgery took less time than the cosmetic surgeries. At 8:30 a.m., I was given a general anesthetic and an epidural. Two hours later, I awoke transformed. It was yet another step on what is a very complex journey. So many steps to get to where I felt I had started, to become what I already was.

Every step I had taken on this journey, from the decision to let my hair grow, to allowing myself to adopt more feminine

So many steps to
get to where I felt I had
started, to become
what I already was.

———————————

mannerisms and clothes, to the surgeries, lessened the dys-phoria I felt. With each step, there was initially fear, but also euphoria and, ultimately, a sense of relief.

"Transgender" is an umbrella category that includes binary and non-binary. There are people who have only a few steps on this journey to find their authentic selves, who feel prop-erly aligned after hormone treatments. There are people who don't feel the need to express primarily as masculine or femi-nine, who are comfortable with traits from each. Some affirm as feminine without having gender-affirming surgery. You know what is right for you when you find peace in your body, heart, and mind. I knew I was someone who would have to fully affirm my female gender to create the proper alignment.

It was incredibly inspiring and humbling to receive hun-dreds of encouraging emails, to have standing ovations. But to say this is an exception is an understatement. Most people who affirm their gender aren't getting onstage to the sound of hun-dreds of cheering people; they aren't getting dozens of emails every day applauding their courage. And not everyone has the financial resources to pursue cosmetic surgery to help them get aligned.

Most transformations come with anxiety; I experienced the greatest outright fear of my life. I was middle-aged when I made my transformation, both an advantage and a disadvantage. I was mature and had more resources at my disposal than the vast majority. I had a support network in place. But at my age, there was also more to undo and a lot of life's complexity to balance.

The feminization surgeries aren't merely cosmetic. The *Journal of the American Medical Association* looked at a cohort of 27,715 transgender people, the largest study in the United States, and found a link between gender-affirming surgeries of any kind and improved mental health.

It is deeply disturbing to me to see how, despite overwhelming medical evidence, more and more US states are moving to ban gender-affirming surgeries. In 2022, 315 anti-2SLGBTQ+ bills were introduced in state legislatures. While less than 10 percent were passed (29), it hasn't stopped the deluge. By the end of February 2023, more than 340 new anti-2SLGBTQ+ bills had been introduced, 150 of them aimed at the transgender community, with the aim of restricting access to gender-affirming care. Most of these bills were directed at minors, but at least four states introduced bills restricting care for adults. My heart hurts deeply for those who are prevented from resolving their dysphoria, or who don't receive the love and support from family, friends, or colleagues. My heart hurts for those who battle mental health challenges, and for the beautiful lives lost to suicide.

The Human Rights Campaign had anticipated 2023 would be "historically bad" for 2SLGBTQ+ people. It is sad and disturbing that here we are, over a quarter of the way into the twenty-first century, and we have regressed to a point not seen in decades. It feels like a war against 2SLGBTQ+ people.

Every war produces casualties. In this case, they won't be visible to the general population. But inside millions of homes, there will be anguish and grief and frustration, and in some cases, death, as suicide rates reflect the new legislation. This war is motivated by ideology rather than science, kindness, and empathy, and by fear, and a lack of knowledge. And like so many wars, it is tragic and expensive and unnecessary.

WHEN I CAME OUT, I was extremely privileged and humbled beyond words: I was experiencing a level of freedom, joy, and peace that was beyond anything I could have imagined. I had the love and support of friends and family. I had the support and embrace of thousands of colleagues in and outside of the bank.

In the movie *Eat Pray Love*, Elizabeth Gilbert (played by Julia Roberts) is on a journey to find her truth and self-love. It's the kind of meaningful journey each of us deserves to take. In Rome, Elizabeth and her friend Sofi (played by Tuva Novotny), embrace their bodies and "muffin tops," buying "bigger" jeans that fit. Elizabeth admires a gorgeous silk nightie, and Sofi says, "You should get it." Feeling lonely, Elizabeth says, "For whom?" And Sofi answers, "For yourself." Later, Elizabeth goes back to the store and buys the gorgeous silk nightie for herself. Like Elizabeth, I was finally able to begin to embrace and express myself fully, all of me, *just for me.*

I also began another new journey—living and being in the world fully as a woman. While Katherine was always in me from childhood and I had a deep appreciation and empathy for women, a deep appreciation of things and experiences that were more feminine (versus masculine), I was now living my truth openly and publicly. I was learning for the first time how to navigate this new world as myself, a woman. Little did I know all I would learn and appreciate as a woman, and as a human being, over the coming months and years.

Perspective

Leadership for
the Future

6

InclusionDialogues: Human Lessons

*We must let go of the life we have planned, so as to accept
the one that is waiting for us. Find a place inside where
there's joy and the joy will burn out the pain. Follow your
bliss and the doors will open where there were only walls.*

JOSEPH CAMPBELL

As I MENTIONED, after I came out to more than eighty
thousand colleagues, friends, and family, I received a
flood of emails. Hundreds of people applauded my
courage and offered love and support. But there were also
those who shared their own stories, ones they had been afraid
to share before. There were gay men who told me about their
difficulties in coming out to work colleagues; there were people
with transgender children or nieces or nephews. There were
people who struggled with mental health issues, with learning
disabilities, with their weight. There were people from racial-
ized communities.

People I worked with, clients, executives in other companies and industries, and others approached me in person, too,
to share their stories and struggles. My story, openness, and

vulnerability became a lightning rod for all that we carry inside. I became a safe place where people could feel seen, heard, and appreciated. People approached me and talked about abusive childhoods, alcoholic fathers, the suicides of their family members or friends. An Indigenous woman told me about the racism she had experienced, the devastation of the residential school system, and her struggles with cultural identity. She had watched her family live in shame and fear and pain, and she carried all this inside. It was both humbling and illuminating to get a glimpse into the burdens carried by so many people.

One man told me that the reason he never spoke up in meetings was that he was self-conscious about his accent. A woman from the Caribbean told me the island she lived on had more churches per square kilometre than anywhere else in the world. She also told me that gay men were beaten to death just because of their sexual orientation. She had a gay uncle who moved to Canada to avoid persecution and publicly lived as a straight man until his death from AIDS. A gay cousin went to live in France to avoid violence at home.

The best weapon against this kind of prejudice and hurt is to drag it into the light in kind, safe, and judgement-free environments. The more people who are publicly out with their story, the more it becomes normalized. It is a long and very bumpy, sometimes dangerous road, but at some point, we will reach the end if we just keep marching. It is very hard to not love when we are upfront and personal with others.

I've always been curious about the human journey, about human struggle. It may be partly because of my parents growing up in the war and being in prison camps, and partly because we were relatively poor farmers. I was trying to figure myself out—who I was innately, my essence. I've come to feel, see, and understand my love of humanity. I have a love of human beings at their best... when we act out of kindness, love, and empathy.

It blew me away to have thousands of people now telling me their stories of hurt and hardship. I was, and continue to be, deeply humbled by it.

Joseph Campbell, who popularized the concept of the hero's journey, said, "Opportunities to find deeper powers within ourselves come when life seems most challenging." This was how InclusionDialogues began, when the Black Lives Matter movement was ramping up and COVID-19 was happening. We required a whole other level of care and compassion for the vulnerabilities that clients and employees were experiencing than we had seen before in the business world. I observed that most companies were going out and taking a reactive approach: They would launch a fund to support Black entrepreneurs, or create a course to support Indigenous truth and reconciliation in response to the horrific media coverage of residential school trauma, abuse, and deaths.

My view was that it's good and important for companies to do these things, but it's not enough. And so InclusionDialogues was born. I created a platform for profiling the voices and experiences of marginalized groups and anyone who had triumphed over unimaginable hardship and deep hurt. My aim in hosting these conversations, which were organized as video calls, was to show the "visible and invisible dimensions of human uniqueness" that we each carry and to model how leaders can hold their own inclusion dialogues within their teams. Talks like these hadn't really happened in the banking world before. I wanted to help create judgement- and fear-free environments where everyone could feel heard, seen, and appreciated for who they are and all they have the potential to bring to others and the mission of their team or organization.

Note: Asking individuals to share vulnerable parts of themselves with others, let alone with thousands of people, is a very delicate and sensitive matter. It must be their choice to do so, and they must want to do it freely. In this book, I have changed the names of those I interviewed unless they gave permission to be named. No one should ever be put in a position where they feel compelled to share parts of themselves when they are not ready or don't want to. It's also important to have professional support available should the need arise.

I heard about harrowing experiences, about grief. The stories came from the community, colleagues, clients, and employees. Their experiences gave them the resilience to become who they are now. Our past shapes us, but it doesn't define us. Many of us carry intergenerational trauma. I shared their stories because they were inspirational and gave us courage to face our own journey with less fear and greater peace; they brought us closer to our truth, our unique gifts.

I was motivated to create open business environments where people could be free and vulnerable with each other as a way of building trust, teamwork, mutual respect, and understanding. I asked people, in a very kind, respectful way, where particular attributes they had came from—whether it was a fear of making a decision or they were hyper-independent, for example. Everyone I spoke with had hurt and hardship stories. I found that once I knew their childhood story, once I knew who they were more deeply, I was able to understand their behaviour and why they did what they did in times of strength, but also in times of vulnerability. It allowed me to be a more empathic leader. It allowed me to understand where people's gifts came from.

Increasingly, people began to recommend speakers to me who had profound stories. Every month or two, I interviewed someone who was highly respected in business yet had never shared their story. I would ask three or four basic questions in a kind, judgement-free environment. I'd start with, "Tell us a bit about who you are today and what you've achieved in your life." And then I would ask them about their journey through hurt or hardship. I'd ask what they hoped for and wanted others to learn and do differently... leaders and all. Hundreds of colleagues witnessed never-heard-before life experiences, often in tears, feeling the deepest levels of empathy and understanding. The psychological safety and sense of belonging across twenty-five thousand colleagues grew significantly, as did client loyalty and other positive business results.

One of the people I interviewed for InclusionDialogues was "Mary," an Indigenous woman born in northern Manitoba. Her biological mother had gone into the residential school system in the Northwest Territories after her own mother had died. The first school she was in burned down, and while she was in the second school, her father died and her siblings were scattered across the prairies. At the school, Mary's mother prayed twice a day. In her child's mind, she thought they were praying about the bad things that some of the priests and nuns did to them. She thought the school was a kind of prison, which it effectively was. They had limited time to play outside, bedtime was very early, and they were not allowed to talk in their traditional language. She was always hungry, she told Mary. And they weren't allowed to leave.

When she was finally released from the school, years later, after suffering torment and abuse, she had no family. Her parents were dead and she had no way of finding any of her siblings. She had no identification and didn't even know her real name. The nuns had called her Martha. Some of the children received only numbers.

Mary's mother fell in love with an Indigenous man who shared that he had also been in a residential school. They didn't get married because Mary's mother still didn't have any identification—they couldn't legally marry. It was almost a decade later that she found out her real age and her name: Anna.

"My mother's experience in residential schools left her ill-equipped to be a parent," Mary told me. "She didn't know how to be a mother or know what a family should be. She left us when I was six months old. My father married a woman from Winnipeg who was not Indigenous just because he wanted to find someone who would be a good mother to me and my sister. He didn't love her. After three years, he knew it just wouldn't work, and he was going to take my sister and [me]. But she said, 'I need to adopt Mary, I've had her since she was little.' So she adopted me and my father left." Mary's sister didn't get along with the adoptive mother and left home, so it was just the two of them. Mary's adoptive mother also had a son who was three years older than Mary. He did not get along with her adoptive mother either; he left home at thirteen years old and moved in with her sister.

Her adoptive mother was going to nursing school, so they had no money. There often wasn't any food in the refrigerator. "When she graduated from nursing school, she took me shopping. I was thirteen. She wanted to buy a dress for the graduation ceremony. In front of the sales clerk, I said, 'What about groceries?' I was worried we wouldn't have food if she bought that dress. She sometimes wrote bad cheques at the grocery store. She was angry with me, but it was always like I was in survival mode growing up."

A year later, her adoptive mother left her, taking a nursing job in the north. Mary was fourteen, still in high school. She was working two jobs, one of them at a hotel that had a popular bar at the south end of Winnipeg. Food had been scarce in their home, but after her mother left, food became even scarcer. Thankfully, Mary had friends. She shared an apartment with a few roommates.

Now, let's pause a moment in the story and consider that when I met her, Mary was a top-talent employee working in a call centre as an assistant manager. I met her at a town hall. She was radiant and had this wonderful, magnetic energy about her. I remember she was deeply curious and not afraid to ask profound questions. So I zoned in, thinking, *Who is this person?*

If I hadn't asked her story, I wouldn't have known that Mary had once been, essentially, a homeless orphan who put herself through high school on Kraft Dinner and ketchup.

"It was just terrible," Mary said. While she didn't experience much racism (though her sister, who looked more Indigenous, did), she was acutely aware of her poverty, living on rice, pasta, and ketchup and wearing second-hand clothes. Her teachers didn't see her as someone who would succeed in life and she was marginalized at school. "I was one of those kids in high school labelled 'least likely to succeed,'" she told me.

After graduating, Mary worked various retail jobs. Like many high school graduates, she didn't know what she wanted to do with her life, didn't know what she could do. At the age of eighteen, she met her birth mother for the first time. "I was so nervous and excited," she said. "I asked my father to come with me. It was a very disappointing experience. She regretted leaving my father and pretty much ignored me and paid more attention to him. It was heartbreaking. I left that meeting devastated and angry. I vowed never to see her again. It was like she left me again." Thirty-one years went by before they saw one another again.

In that time, Mary got a job at a bank, which had an Indigenous program available. They were trying to increase representation within the bank and had hired Mary as an Elder to advise them. She didn't stay at the bank but changed jobs and rose quickly through the corporate ranks. She got married, started a family.

Her adult life bore no resemblance to her childhood. All its outward traces were gone. But the memories of that time, that person, remained.

When Mary's daughter was in grade 12, she did a project on residential schools and interviewed Mary's birth mother without Mary knowing. "My daughter knew I wouldn't have approved of her recording a telephone interview with my biological mother, whom I hadn't spoken to in thirty years. And she knew I wouldn't want my mother's story to be heard by others, given what she experienced in the residential school." But Mary's daughter played the recording for the class. It had been edited; after taking out the worst stories of abuse, the twenty-minute conversation was only five minutes long. Still, by the end of the recording, the whole class was crying.

A year later, Mary met her birth mother again. It was an emotional experience. "Neither of us could bear to talk about why she left me. But after that meeting, I truly found forgiveness and I was finally at peace."

A week after that reunion, Mary finally listened to the recording her daughter had made a year earlier. "I could only listen to the edited version," Mary said. "I didn't want to hear the really bad stuff. I know what happened in those schools. It was very difficult for me to listen to my seventy-year-old mother crying, telling her story about her experience, and to hear her say her heart has never healed and she has not forgotten the atrocities she experienced."

The trauma that Mary experienced is extraordinary, dating back generations, from first contact with Europeans centuries ago through the treaties issued under our first prime minister, John A. Macdonald, and finally, her parents' experience in residential schools. The first residential school in Canada was created in 1831, though the term usually refers to those federally established, after 1880. The last one, Kivalliq Hall in Rankin Inlet, didn't close until 1997, meaning more than a century of torment, families being split apart, a culture under assault with the intent of eradicating it, physical and sexual abuse. There are more than five thousand school representatives who have been identified as abusers.

In addition, thousands of Indigenous children died at these schools—mass graves have been discovered. Their parents never knew what became of them, never knew they died, or when, or where. And the nightmarish graves have reawakened the trauma that thousands of residential school survivors tried to bury. There is catharsis with the public recognition of the extent of the horrors that they endured, but there is also the tearing open of old wounds.

Despite having two Indigenous parents, Mary didn't have "Indian status," which meant she wasn't recognized by the government. She hadn't grown up on a reservation, and didn't know where her parents had grown up before they entered the residential school system. "I didn't have a culture," she said. "I didn't even know which community I was from or where my mother had been before residential school." She was stranded between cultures, without the support of a family and without friends. She was spectacularly alone.

"Over the years," Mary said, "I came to the conclusion that the adversity I faced as a child gave me strength, courage, and perseverance. That adversity built my resiliency and made me more empathic to others. It helped me find forgiveness for all three of my parents. My childhood experience made me the person I am today and for that I am grateful... So I dreamed big and I didn't let my past define me. I changed my path."

Mary is now vice president of a large corporation. She climbed higher than she ever imagined she would, much higher

She was stranded
between cultures, without
the support of a family
and without friends. She
was spectacularly alone.

---

than her teachers imagined. "My family was broken," she said, "but I was very fortunate to find a mentor at work. She had a belief in me and what was possible when others didn't. Without her, I would not have found total forgiveness and peace in my life. She saw me for who I am—my whole self. She changed my path. She helped me build an inclusive world for Indigenous people and all forms of diversity [and] uniqueness in my role as a leader.

"We have a responsibility to create a workplace where all employees feel they belong and they can bring their whole selves to work. We all need to feel safe to speak up and share our stories."

I couldn't agree more. I was seeing the business world shift and change—for the better. At first, creating gentle space for people to share their story, in an environment of no judgement, resulted in shock, but that quickly became empathy for and understanding of people with different lived experiences. It resulted in a freer, easier and harmonious environment for working and solving problems in a much more holistic way.

InclusionDialogues were meant to showcase role models. I wanted to show not their material world definition of success but rather the fact that these role models—the most kind, empathic, and resilient people—all had hardship in their background. And the basic message was if you are dealing with any hurt and hardship, you are not alone. These experiences became the gifts that help make these role models the deep and value-based human beings they are.

Mary's experiences gave her resilience, determination, and kindness that distinguished her as a human being, a woman, and an extraordinary leader.

I saw then that the more I did empathy and vulnerability sessions, and the more we told stories and held inclusion dialogues, the more people felt psychologically safe, had hope, felt belonging, felt comfortable leaning in and speaking up. I wanted to create hope for those who were the most isolated and struggling. I wanted to bring people together in ways they had never been before to solve some of the most pressing and complex problems of our time.

"SUSAN'S" STORY is another of the dozens I heard, one that is all too familiar to many who have lived in abusive households. When I met her, I saw someone determined, independent, and with a real warmth about her. I went out of my way to get to know her. Everybody who knew her in the community thought she had extraordinary potential. One time when we were together, the topic of family came up. I inquired a bit about her upbringing, and I was fairly open about the fact that my parents had been prisoners, survivors of war, and that this trauma had extended into my childhood home.

Susan opened up, too, and told me that she had grown up in a small village in Saskatchewan and was the oldest child of three in her family (she had a younger brother and sister). Their home was on acreage, so there were no immediate neighbours—no witnesses. Susan assumed they were a normal family because she had no real experience of other families. It would be years before she realized what happened in their home wasn't normal.

"My father was a severe alcoholic," Susan said. "Power and control were very important to him. We grew up in a world where what happens in your family is not to be shared. You didn't talk about it. Growing up, we were this perfect family of three children and a mom and a dad." Her father had a good job. They had a nice house.

"But my earliest memory is waking up and hearing slapping against the wall and knowing it was my mom being beaten. Dad would come home, and I could hear this, it was always a kind of thud, thud, thud. I could hear him yelling at her, telling her she was like a dog. I was always waking up to these sounds. She would spend nights under the bed in fear." The kids would also huddle in their beds, terrified.

"In grade three, I remember getting caught playing with matches on the football field. My punishment was my fingertips were burned. My father held a match to them until they blistered. My mom had a look of horror on her face. I was told that the next time this happened, my father would burn my whole hand, that it would go on the burner of the stove. And at the time, you just think, well, that was our family, it's kind of how you grow up."

Both the verbal and physical abuse increased as her father's alcohol addiction got worse. When Susan's maternal grandfather died, it gave her father licence to be more abusive. "My sister woke me up in the middle of the night, and said, 'Something's going on.' I opened the door to my parents' bedroom and my dad had a pillow over my mom's face. He was choking her."

According to Susan, when he saw the kids at the door, he chased them downstairs. He yelled and threatened them. He hit the children, though not the way he hit his wife. "To this day, I still wake up being chased down the stairs," Susan said. "My heart races and I wake up."

As a teenager, Susan began to rebel, standing up to her father. One day, when he was assaulting her mother, she told him to stop and he grabbed her and held her arms. She screamed in his face, "I will never be like you!"

Her mother was a kind and caring person, but she lived in constant fear of her husband's temper and the threat of violence. At one point, she tried to get away. One of Susan's siblings woke her up in the middle of the night because there were sounds coming from outside the house. The kids knew the sounds meant something bad. Susan's sister told her she had to do something: She was the oldest. Susan flew down the stairs. It was winter, and Susan put her boots on and her jacket over her pajamas. Her parents were outside on the driveway. Her mom was in the car, trying to drive away, and her father was blocking the driveway. "I looked at my dad, and I could see his hand was full of blood," Susan said. "He was hitting the window, trying to break it, then he lay on the hood of the car. My mother revved the engine. She was inside the car, sobbing. When my father saw me, he saw red. He was completely irrational, like he wasn't there. He grabbed me by the neck and threw me onto the hood of the car. That was the only time I thought, 'I don't know if I'm going to get out of this one.' Mom eventually opened the door."

Their father finally went inside the house and slept it off. Another battle ended, everyone's adrenaline slowly subsiding.

The lessons of Susan's childhood were harsh and stayed with her. "We learned as a family how to protect each other and help each other. The four of us became really, really tight."

By the age of seventeen, she had taken on the role of the family's protector. "There was a situation where it got really ugly," Susan recalled when I interviewed her. "I had just graduated from high school. I was seventeen. The evening went really, really bad. He came home and was abusive. My mom had a blue Ford Tempo, and I put my sister in the passenger seat and my mom and brother in the back seat, and we put everything we possibly could in this little car. I didn't know where the hell I was going, but I knew we were getting out of there. My father ripped all the wiring out of the automatic garage door opener so we couldn't get the garage door open. The police ended up coming and taking him in to the police station. My mom refused to press charges, but I pressed charges. My mom was almost comatose, she was non-responsive. I remember getting into the vehicle and driving west and thinking, *I don't know where we're going.*"

Susan's mother and her siblings returned to the family home after seeking support from a women's shelter. Susan stayed with her grandmother for a brief time and never moved back. Eventually, her parents divorced, but her father remained a manipulative force in their lives. At her wedding, Susan refused to let her father walk her down the aisle. She walked alone.

There was never a reconciliation, but after her father stopped drinking, there was acceptance. She allowed her father to see and build a relationship with his grandson. Her father died during the height of COVID-19.

It was years after Susan left home that she understood that her upbringing wasn't in any way normal. The trauma of her childhood and adolescence left a mark. But it had also made her resilient and independent. She had seen her mother bullied and resolved to never let that happen to her.

Susan climbed to the top of the corporate ladder and now works as a president for a large corporation, but it wasn't an easy climb. "People would say, 'You know, Susan, we think you have something to offer, but we never hear your voice.' What was holding me back? What was I really afraid of?"

As soon as I heard Susan's story, I thought, "I now know you. I now know why you do what you do. It's what you did to survive." She exudes warmth and love, which is her essence, but there's also this survivor in her—a deeply independent, quietly determined individual.

Susan and I talked about how these are the kinds of stories we need to hear. We have to uncover the whole individual in order to understand them, see their gifts, and support and embrace them. She had been physically abused by her father but had conditioned herself to never cry. She had witnessed horror in the family but had been told never to tell anyone the family's business. This is something that many people have been conditioned to do, especially those of us who grew up during the 1970s.

Shaped by her hardships, Susan went on to become a wonderful mother, spouse, and successful leader. I mentored her for many years. She's someone who has created safe spaces for others. Susan's experiences gave her the resilience, determination, and kindness that have shaped the incredible woman and leader she is today.

ANOTHER STORY came from "Robert," who grew up in eastern Canada. I observed Robert continually taking on challenge after challenge after challenge and conquering each one. Robert was always working with and advocating for people—underprivileged people in the community, customers of his business, employees—and putting his neck on the line. Over time, I got to see a 360-degree view of Robert being all in with everybody, and his high level of fearlessness.

He opened up to me about how his mother's mental illness had left an indelible mark. "She was suffering from depression," Robert said. "Severe depression coupled with agoraphobia." Her first bout of depression came after giving birth to Robert. When he was a child, she often reminded him that her depression had begun with his birth. "She said many times that it started with me, so over time, [I] feel guilt."

Robert's mother went in and out of her depression, but it progressed over the years. "In her twenties, she had an episode, then a bit more in her thirties, and a bit more in her forties. And the year she turned fifty, that was the lowest time. And her way of dealing with the suffering was to end the suffering." She died by suicide, leaving a devastated family when Robert was twenty-four.

She and Robert's father were part of what sociologists call "the silent generation." They didn't talk about their problems. Robert's mother didn't see a psychiatrist. His father refused to acknowledge her illness. "Mental health [help], for him, was only for crazy people and crazy people were institutionalized, and he certainly didn't see his wife in that category. It took us many years to overcome the guilt of not being able to support her, and the guilt of not being able to even recognize the reality."

Robert's difficult childhood left him with valuable lessons for leadership, though. "As a leader, you try to go beyond what you see on the surface and show not just empathy, but support. If you refuse to see a problem, usually it just grows. I think my childhood and difficult experiences I had with my mother shaped me as a human being and a leader." Like Susan and Mary, Robert developed resilience, determination, and kindness, which he brings to all aspects of his life.

His parents' refusal to talk about their problems was something I could definitely relate to. After hearing his story, I came realize that what Robert was really doing in his business approach was not leaving anyone behind. Robert was innately wired to fearlessly advocate for those who couldn't fight or advocate for themselves.

Sometimes, Robert would get overwhelmed because he felt the weight of the world on his shoulders. I would say, "Robert, you're okay. I see you." "You know," he'd say, "I'm really frustrated." And I would respond, "You're not alone, I've got your back." His anxiety would diminish and he would return to the place where his experiences became a gift—that of seeing potential in others and having the courage to advocate.

Robert was incredibly smart. All the individuals I interviewed were smart, talented people, from an intellectual standpoint. All had a certain level of education, but it wasn't about that. That's not what determined their impact. *Impact* is a better word than success, because the impact is about making a difference. Success is something that can be measured in financial or materialistic terms. Impact is about something deeper and more holistic.

DURING THE ISOLATION of the COVID-19 pandemic, I connected with "Marieke" through LinkedIn and the life coaching business she was promoting. Before COVID, she had been an expedition leader for tours of Antarctica. I was inspired by Marieke and her story of courage, specifically the courage to save herself.

Marieke had been living in the Netherlands, in a small town outside of Amsterdam, and working as a psychologist for autistic children and troubled teenagers. She was also in a very unhealthy, abusive relationship, which she finally ended. "I remember breaking that off," she said, "because the fear of staying was greater than the fear of the unknown. People stay in relationships because they are terrified of the unknown." But at some point, the fear of staying became greater for her.

Leaving that relationship, Marieke suddenly had the desire to travel, to get out and see more of the world. She decided to go to Nepal and hike through the Himalayas for a month. It was scary to be out on her own, but it was also a deeply fulfilling experience. At the end of the hike, she met an Australian man and fell in love, and made the decision to leave her family, job, and country to move to the other side of the planet.

Unfortunately, that relationship turned into an unhealthy situation as well, as her husband became increasingly difficult. In the course of the relationship, she worked as an expedition guide in remote places she'd never been. "It helped me to embrace things that were out of my comfort zone," she said. "You can only build confidence when you do things out of your comfort zone. I love my comfort zone. But I learned to step out of it."

Her husband became verbally abusive, and she felt she deserved better, but it was when he became physically abusive that she found the courage to leave. When she left him, she left everything—their two properties, her possessions. "I literally had two suitcases. I gave everything away. I didn't want to have anything that reminded me of that marriage anymore. I wanted to start from scratch with nothing. I was happy that I could truly build my own life and create something for myself that I'm proud of."

At the time, Marieke was a middle-aged woman, far from friends or family, but she had some experience as an expedition leader, and she looked for a job in that area. She found one, which took her around the world. She was leading people in remote, often harsh conditions. "We are in the most remote places, like Antarctica. You don't have hospitals nearby. You don't have help nearby. You're dealing with natural elements that you cannot control. You have two hundred people on board the ship and a team of twenty-five people that you have to lead."

It was a big adjustment, but Marieke found a new life for herself, one that was on her terms. "When I think back about my life," she said, "I [see I] was so attached to security. I had no idea that I would ever live like this, that I would travel around the world, that I would have no home, that everything you would relate to security, I don't have. But I love that I always live in a way that is adventurous. You never really know what tomorrow is going to bring. It's vital we learn to listen to our intuition and heart, and not our fear-based mind."

When Marieke and I met online and had video calls, we immediately hit it off, recognizing some of the similarities in our journeys, the challenges we had faced, and the confidence we had gained in facing those challenges. "Confidence is something you need to build by doing something that is scary," she said. "That takes courage. You can start with something small, then do something bigger. But then something that stretches you, something that is scary but you face it and do it anyway."

Today, Marieke not only leads expeditions in Antarctica but also coaches expedition leaders and teams across her entire company and throughout the world. Through her resilience and determination, and her kindness and empathy, she has demonstrated leadership that brings out the best in others; leadership that creates psychological safety and belonging, that allows people to take risks, to learn and work in ways that yield incredible results. As my friend and author Dr. Robyne Hanley-Dafoe says, "We can do hard things."

The idea behind InclusionDialogues was that hearing people's stories helps others feel less alone in this world. And when people see that hardship can lead to greatness, the stories give them the hope, love, and resilience to endure and heal, and the courage to grow and become more aligned with their gifts and true potential. It helps people become more resilient, determined, kind, and closer to their bliss.

The Japanese art of repairing pottery with gold, called *kintsugi*, is a well-known metaphor for things that are made more beautiful for having been broken. While the word "broken" may elicit a negative reaction, the truth is that trauma divides a person inside; it prevents them from being who they want to be. Suffering through hardship requires healing to help one feel more whole. And those who have experienced and come through and have healed their trauma are more unique and beautiful. Often, the kindest and most resilient individuals have experienced the most, have grown the most, and give the most. They would never want another human being to experience what they have.

IN THE COURSE OF hearing others' stories, and their anxieties and fears, I got to know them better, on a deeper level. One of the greatest honours of my life has been to be utterly trusted by people, and to be able to see, embrace, and support the whole person. I did this inside and outside of work for more than twenty-five years, maybe because of my deep curiosity about the human condition, or maybe because I was trying to figure myself out too. I learned to be open and vulnerable myself.

The dialogues helped me understand that my own resilience and determination were part of a coping mechanism to deal with trauma. I learned that there was a deeper part of myself that I began to explore, both part of and separate from my gender truth. Learning about others helped me know myself; they helped me get to peace with myself.

I had beat myself up for decades because I didn't think or solve problems the way many corporate executives do, which is in a very linear, logical, methodical way. I am a non-linear thinker, and it took me till my early to mid-fifties to understand that my mind was just wired differently. I didn't know what dyslexia was. I didn't understand neurodiversity. I thought I was broken.

I didn't know what
dyslexia was. I didn't
understand neurodiversity.
I thought I was broken.

———————————

Jack Mezirow, author of *Transformative Dimensions of Adult Learning*, introduces us to the concept of "disorienting dilemmas," or challenging and "unexpected incidents." He helps us see how these challenges and hardships create the conditions for us to be humbled and ultimately learn and grow, and adjust our understanding of ourselves and the world around us.

So again, not only can people do hard things, but it is the hard things that can help us develop extraordinary levels of determination, resilience, empathy, compassion, and kindness—character. This helps us become skilled and talented leaders within organizations and society. Everyone in society can be a leader, a role model, a caregiver for others and our world. Fred Kofman, founder and president of Conscious Business Center International, appropriately said, "Wisdom without compassion is ruthlessness and compassion without wisdom is folly."

My coming out served to amplify this lesson. It exposed me to the lived experience of fear or hurt that causes people to hold back their potential. It taught me that diversity is all around us—that diversity is both invisible and visible dimensions of human uniqueness. And that uniqueness is shaped by each person's experiences and intersectionality, all of the inherited and lived layers of a person. Inclusivity happens when we each feel true belonging and psychological safety. With inclusivity, each person is able to more easily take "the hero's journey" or "disorienting dilemma" and move through their fears and hurt to find and bring more of their full potential and unique *beauty* to their life, to society, to their work, and to our world.

The first time I ever saw myself. New York, 2019.

The day after seeing myself for the first time.
Here, I did my own makeup.

Giving the keynote address at the Canadian Museum for Human Rights. Winnipeg, 2021.

In my element and as my whole self—corporate mode.

New Year's at my friends Joe and Andreas's place, 2022.

Celebrating my birthday in New York, 2023.

Peloponnese, Greece, 2023.

Bonding with a horse that unexpectedly came over to me in the Dolomites, spring 2022.

Joy in the Dolomites, Italy, with my friends.

Ready for the next adventure.

7

The 2SLGBTQ+ Community and Mental Health

———————————

What mental health needs is more sunlight, more candor, and more unashamed conversation.

GLENN CLOSE

IN JUNE 2021, for Pride Month, I gave a talk to the employees and volunteers of Kids Help Phone. My own mental health issues had spiked before I came out, which is maybe why I led with vulnerability and making the video about my story.

Our definition of love is framed by our relationship with our parents. My dad would scream and yell, and then when he was drunk, he'd offer us money. Or he'd buy me treats when we went to pick up stuff for the mink at the abattoir. But it meant there was this hot-cold relationship with my father. And while I had this deeply compassionate connection with my mother, I also had a similar hot-cold relationship with her because she would go out to the farm to work for hours, leaving me alone in the house as a small child. This relationship with my parents produced what psychologists call an anxious attachment style, which created in me a fear of abandonment.

So when I came out, what spiked in my psyche was this fear. As I said before, a therapist diagnosed me in the 97th percentile for anxiety. Every human being experiences life through three lenses—their cultural background, their gender or whatever spectrum they're on, and their life traumas—the fears that we carry from our early life as a baby to experiencing upsets in our adult life. We build coping mechanisms around them. Thankfully, by the time I was asked to speak on mental health, I was well on my way with my own healing journey.

Canada has the third-highest suicide rate in the developed world. Every day, more than two hundred Canadians attempt suicide; twelve people die by suicide, approximately 4,400 deaths per year. Suicide rates among men are three times higher than among women. The mental health pandemic affects everyone: women, men, and teens. Suicide is the second-leading cause of death for young people aged fifteen to twenty-four. One in seven people in that age group have reported having suicidal thoughts. And who knows how many others have those thoughts but aren't reporting. And we know that marginalized groups experience higher degrees of social and economic exclusion and of course experience the stress and mental health issues that follow. Mental health is vital to a healthy society, but for decades mental illness was under-reported and largely ignored, and mental health was underfunded and stigmatized. People would often hide their mental health challenges and find ways to cope without support. And now we face a crisis, a mental health pandemic that has no easy solution.

Governments have been slow to address the problem of mental health in general, and suicide in particular. One of the problems is that mental health is complex, encompassing so many different causes, conditions, and outcomes. Suicide is the most tragic of those outcomes. In that gap left by government, organizations have formed that offer both help and hope. One of those organizations is Kids Help Phone, which was established more than thirty years ago and has grown into Canada's only 24-7 mental health service, offering free, confidential, multilingual support to young people. Each year, Kids Help Phone deals with youth between the ages of five and twenty-nine. In 2021, it handled 4.6 million calls across all service channels, an average of 12,300 every day. In 2022, that figure increased: By then, 22 percent of calls involved suicide. It was the fourth most common issue, behind anxiety, relationships, and depression.

Kids Help Phone is one of the best sources of data on youth mental health, and that data demonstrates the vast scope of the problem, a problem that intensified during the COVID-19 pandemic. In 2022, Kids Help Phone logged the highest number of interactions ever, with a 250 percent increase in phone interactions, and a 78 percent increase in texting over 2019 volume. The people contacting Kids Help Phone wanted to talk about anxiety, stress, relationships, suicidal ideation, eating disorders, sexual abuse, bulling, grief, and isolation, among other issues.

The talk I gave to the organization's employees and volunteers across the country was by video. We were in the middle of the pandemic, and all the June Pride parades had been cancelled. One of the great benefits of those parades is the visibility. We see large numbers of diverse people publicly celebrated and cheered. But in the second year of the pandemic, what we had was continued isolation. People weren't seeing anyone like themselves. It was one more blow against 2SLGBTQ+ youth, who account for about 55 percent of texting conversations with Kids Help Phone. In 2021, the average interaction with texters to the helpline was forty-four minutes, an indication of how isolated young people felt during this time, how badly they needed contact and understanding.

So I wanted to reinforce the idea that there were others like them out there, that I had gone through a very dark period but had come out the other side, and they could too. Stories are important; they're how we shape a culture. And without cultural touchstones like the Pride parade, they are more important than ever.

I told them about my years of torment and confusion, my thoughts of ending my life. It's only by bringing mental health out into the light that we can make any headway. We want to create a generation of people who see mental health as a health and wellness issue, a generation that isn't stigmatized by mental health issues.

I know what it feels like to experience episodes of severe anxiety and depression. I was very lucky—it wasn't like I was living in depression for days or months on end. I just had periods of it. My first severe episode was around New Year in 2019. I had been drinking and a few things happened that really triggered my dysphoria and fear of rejection.

Unfortunately, what often happens in these situations is that friends and family don't understand and tell you to "snap out of it." And you can't just snap out of it. You know you're supposed to, and you want to, but you can't. It isn't for lack of trying.

Later, in the fall of 2022, I went through a mild relapse and another journey... this time an inner journey. It was a period of deep grief, shame, and sadness—nothing like what I had experienced when I was suicidal in the fall of 2018. Thankfully, because I began living in alignment with myself, with my truth, I've never really gone back into that kind of depression or had such severe anxiety. But the reason that minor relapse occurred was that I did still have healing to do around my fears of abandonment and rejection. It was really the beginning of my deeper spiritual journey, rather than my psychological journey. At that point, I embraced reading about spiritual practices, the untethered soul. I began meditating to Joe Dispenza, who's a *New York Times* bestselling author, researcher, corporate consultant, and lecturer.

From 2018 to my coming out, I coped. In 2022, I learned to be alone with myself. I learned to decompress in solitude. I learned to balance how much time I was putting myself out there in the world with how much time I needed to just rest and decompress.

Aside from meditating, I began to embrace deeper mental health and spiritual practices. I hired a tantric coach to gain more awareness in body. Later, in the fall of 2023, I hired a life coach. This helped me tune into my essence and the things that make me unique beyond gender.

The game changer for me and my mental health was rest—and healing—and an inner journey, different modalities of healing to allow me to know and fully step into my essence and life as Katherine. I had to fully integrate all of my life experiences—life in a man's world, life in a woman's world, my neurodiversity, life as a child, and life in the corporate world. All of my wellness practices created the space for me to fully integrate myself.

It's funny how sometimes it takes us our whole lives to get to this place where we can just *be*. The first phase of my journey was an outer path to *becoming* Katherine. The second phase was an inner journey to my essence, to *being* Katherine.

Another charitable organization I am involved with that addresses the issue of youth mental health is Jack.org. I joined its board in 2020 and am very happy to be involved with such a worthwhile initiative. It was founded by Eric Windeler and his wife, Sandra Hanington. Sadly, Jack.org grew out of a tragedy. In 2010, Eric and Sandra received the devastating news that too

The game changer for me
and my mental health was rest—
and healing. Different modalities
of healing allowed me to
know and fully step into my
essence and life as Katherine.

———————————

many other parents have received. Their son Jack, a first-year student at Queen's University in Kingston, Ontario, had died by suicide.

"If you had asked us in early March of 2010 how we were doing as a family," Eric said to me, "I would have told you we thought we had three happy, healthy children. I was a successful entrepreneur and my wife, Sandra, was a senior executive at one of the Big Five banks. You don't want to find out about mental health the way we did, with a call from a police officer. That gentleman had to come to our house and tragically tell us that they had found our dear son Jack in his residence room. He had died by suicide the night before. We were just flattened, devastated. We didn't even know he was struggling."

This is, unfortunately, a familiar story. "No one was talking about mental health back then," Eric said, "and clearly Jack wasn't comfortable reaching out for support at Queen's or reaching out to us." This underscores the stigma and shame that some youth feel when they are struggling.

In the wake of Jack's death, Eric and Sandra made a significant donation to Kids Help Phone, and Eric left his job and volunteered full time there. While there, he and Sandra launched a pilot program with the aim of identifying a specific gap they could fill in the mental health space, somewhere they could make a difference. They didn't want other parents to have to go through what they did. What they identified was that young people were being left out of the mental health conversation.

"We landed on what we call our youth engagement, youth leadership model, which is based on peer-to-peer education about mental health," Eric said. They started with Queen's University, training young leaders in mental health, and eventually took the program across the country. "If you think of the mental health structure as a pyramid, we're at the bottom, trying to reach and educate all young people about mental health before they're in crisis or struggling, so they learn how to build their own tool kit and take care of their own mental health, keep their eyes on their peers, and feel comfortable about reaching out if they are struggling."

By 2013, Jack.org was established as an independent national charity, and soon after was active in every province and territory. It now has eighty-five full-time staff and more than three thousand young people who volunteer in its peer-to-peer programs. Each year, they train and certify more than one hundred Jack Talk speakers, people between the ages of eighteen and twenty-four, who volunteer to go through forty hours of public speaking training and mental health awareness training. They also learn how to share their own story. Each year, there are several hundred talks at high schools, colleges, universities, and in community settings. Young leaders from Jack.org visit more than seven hundred schools a year. The underlying idea is that young people are most likely to listen and relate to a peer talking about mental health. As the website notes, "In most social movements, we insist that those who are affected speak for themselves. Those who hold the experience hold the space. Yet strangely, when it comes to youth, we often let others do the talking. But youth know themselves best. They know their own issues and obstacles."

At the request of Jack.org's youth network, the organization created an award-winning resource called Be There (bethere .org). This resource teaches young people, and those who support them, about mental health, and trains them how to be there for other young people in a safe and supportive way. Jack .org was contacted by a US-based foundation created by Lady Gaga and her mother, Cynthia Germanotta, and they partnered to create the free and engaging Be There Certificate (bethere certificate.org).

Jack.org not only helps youth help themselves but also educates parents on how to be more aware, more empathetic. As mentioned above, 70 percent of mental illness begins in people between the ages of fifteen and twenty-four. This is a vulnerable time in most people's lives and the right time to address the issue. This organization helps parents and other trusted adults recognize signs of struggle and know how to support the young people in their lives.

Jack.org has matured further with the appointment of a dedicated president and CEO. As the founding family representatives, Eric operates as a founder and Sandra remains on the board.

In 2010, the same year that Jack Windeler died by suicide, Bell launched its Let's Talk initiative with the intention of raising awareness of mental health. Mary Deacon had worked at the Centre for Addiction and Mental Health (CAMH) for almost a decade and was the inaugural president of the CAMH Foundation. She had tried for years to get a large corporation to adopt mental health as its cause of choice. A complex, stigmatized, and wide-ranging issue is a tough sell, and no corporation wanted to take it on. This changed when George Cope became CEO of Bell Canada. He got in touch with Mary and embraced the idea.

"George, like pretty much everyone, including myself," Mary told me, "had a personal interest in mental health. So it was simple for him to grasp the importance of the issue, and he was appalled at the situation we were in, in this affluent, developed country, where people were unable to get the help they need, and that we have such a stigma that keeps people from getting help."

Mary had come to the mental health world through personal experience. Shortly after the birth of her first child, Mary's brother died by suicide at the age of twenty-five. He was a medical student at the University of Toronto. At this point, Mary realized she suffered from depression and sought psychiatric help. Twelve years later, her other brother, Ted, who suffered from depression and obsessive compulsive disorder (OCD) and was living with her, died by suicide at the age of thirty-nine. Mary's own depression never relented, yet she was able to raise two children and become a CEO, a perfect example of what can be achieved when living with mental illness.

The tragedy of her two brothers' deaths and her own clinical depression led Mary into the world of mental health. One of the first goals of the Let's Talk initiative was to reduce the pervasive stigma of mental illness. Their first national spokesperson was Clara Hughes, the only Canadian to have medalled in both the Summer and Winter Olympics (two medals for cycling, four for speed skating). She was the perfect choice. Her winning smile and extraordinary athletic success masked her own battles with depression. Her candour, high profile, and personality helped reduce the stigma. Mary hoped the campaign would start and normalize conversations about mental health.

A conversation did start and is ongoing. Since 2011, more than 1.5 billion messages of support have been shared on Bell Let's Talk Day. "We used the assets we had as a communications company [Bell owns CTV]," Mary said, "to tackle stigma and address a lot of the fallacies and the perception [of] what people with mental illness are like and what they can do. Stigma is the single-largest barrier for people getting treatment. They feel they're alone in their struggle, and showing people who have mental health issues, who are thriving in their lives, is a way to give hope about what is possible."

Stigma is a powerful and stubborn problem in the mental health world, yet little research had been done on it. Mary tried to find academics who were studying the issue and found that there wasn't a single university with a chair or department studying anti-stigma approaches. And not just in Canada—there weren't any in the world. So Bell created their own chair position, and their appointee is the world's leading authority in anti-stigma research. Prior to the creation of the position, this Canadian professor was already a world-leading authority on anti-stigma research. Her appointment as chairperson for Bell Talk enabled her to devote more time and do more research on destigmatization.

Stigma has two essential components: attitudes and behaviours. It is easier to change attitudes than behaviours, and this is where we all have to do our part to understand mental illness as a whole, whether it is affecting a family member or stranger.

But once you get past the stigma and are able to talk about mental illness openly, you still need access to services. And that is also an area that has been sadly lacking in Canada. Bell Let's Talk is focusing on it now. "We have a vision of creating a Canada where everyone can get the mental health support they need to flourish," Mary said. They are trying to make it easier to find services, to reduce wait times, to put together accurate data so we know exactly what we're dealing with, and to measure the effectiveness of the services. To that end, they help fund dozens of organizations, both large and small, including Kids Help Phone and Jack.org.

Bell's Let's Talk has helped create a national conversation about mental health to break down the barriers to understanding and acceptance. As Mary Deacon said, it is a journey, not a destination. There is a long way to go, but initiatives like Jack .org and Bell's Let's Talk, both born out of personal tragedy, have gone a long way toward preventing other tragedies.

I've experienced both the good and dark sides of psychology. When I first started therapy, I was in talk therapy with someone who couldn't relate or empathize. To find the right therapist was a journey of exploration. My strongest therapist was trained as an identity therapist. They did not have a PhD in psychology, but they were the most beautiful, affirming, and aware human being.

From there, I was set up with a psychologist to help Rosemary and me along my journey. She was skillful at helping us navigate our relationship. She knew I was ready to get hormones and letters for surgery. She knew of this gentleman who worked with gender patients. And she set me up with him to get my letters.

It's no longer about suicide for me. I don't think about taking my own life. I don't get depressed or have severe anxiety anymore. If my anxiety gets loud, I meditate. I breathe. If I need to cry, I cry.

When it comes to mental illness, the entire population is at risk, but there are groups that have a higher risk than others: All youth, but especially Indigenous youth and the 2SLGBTQ+ youth community, experience catastrophically high rates of suicidal ideation, suicide attempts, and suicides.

A 2022 national survey in the United States showed that 54 percent of 2SLGBTQ+ teens seriously considered suicide. This was the most extensive survey of its kind, based on interviews with thirty-four thousand 2SLGBTQ+ people aged thirteen to twenty-four. The results were dispiriting, though not unexpected. Among those surveyed, 2SLGBTQ+ teens were six times more likely to experience depression than the general population and 3.5 times more likely to attempt suicide than heterosexual teens. Among transgender teens, the rate was 5.87 times more than the average. Another key statistic: 82 percent wanted mental health care and 60 percent of them were unable to access it. At a time when transgender youth are being persecuted more than they have been in decades, there are fewer mental health care resources available for them. This is a heartbreaking recipe for disaster.

The Movement Advancement Project (MAP), which tracks 2SLGBTQ+ policy, described the current climate, in 2023, as a "war against 2SLGBTQ+ people in America and their very right and ability to openly exist." Many wars (religious, cultural, political) stem from a lack of understanding, which leads to the perception that the other side is somehow less than human and a threat—in this case, a threat to what some lawmakers say are "family values." This term has been used for decades in politics. It tends to be vague and often refers to a 1950s idea of a working father, a stay-at-home mother, and two happy, well-adjusted children. It is a happy fiction, one that has proved to be stubbornly useful in politics.

The reality is that the 2SLGBTQ+ population in the United States is estimated at 20 million, with two million adults identifying as transgender, and certainly many more youth who do. A significant percentage of American families includes 2SLGBTQ+ members. Families are more complex than some lawmakers would like, but in my opinion, you need to address the reality, not the *Leave It to Beaver* version. As in any war, there is needless suffering, there are unforeseen human consequences, and there is economic destruction. From a purely macroeconomic perspective, if the gender diverse community has access to gender-affirming procedures and if the 2SLGBTQ+ population has access to love, kindness, and mental health care, they will be much more psychologically safe and productive, both at work and in their communities.

Being gay or transgender is not a mental health issue. But living with gender dysphoria, fear of judgement and rejection, and potential and/or real discrimination creates the conditions for mental health challenges, including suicide. As Lauren Fogel Mersy said, "Being able to be yourself is one of the strongest components of good mental health."

As the 2SLGBTQ+ community becomes more visible, it is perceived, in some places, to be a threat. Christine Jorgensen was the first public transgender American. In 1952, she went to Denmark to have gender reassignment surgery done because the surgery was not yet available in the United States. She flew back to New York in 1953, landing at Idlewild Airport (now John F. Kennedy International Airport). When she arrived, there were dozens of journalists waiting for her. She took questions, looking glamorous in a fur coat and heels. She was poised and witty and became an instant celebrity.

Her life was relentlessly public. She worked as an actress, singer, and nightclub performer. She was the first visible transgender advocate and was very effective, though her views weren't always welcome. Still, she wasn't ostracized the way the 2SLGBTQ+ community is now. She was seen as an anomaly, not a harbinger of hope and inclusivity.

Publicly, Jorgensen appeared to be happy and well-adjusted, but in her bestselling book, *Christine Jorgensen: A Personal Autobiography*, she described her struggles with depression and thoughts of suicide. "The answer to the problem must not lie in sleeping pills and suicides that look like accidents," she wrote, "but rather in life and the freedom to live it."

She was right, but even now, so many years later, the freedom to live life as a transgender person is still elusive for many.

The 2SLGBTQ+ community in the United States is under severe pressure politically, but the corporate world has been much more progressive. Ninety-six percent of Forbes 500 companies have non-discrimination policies that include sexual orientation, and 71 percent have policies that include transgender people. Hope exists in corporations that understand that their clients and workforce of the future are our youth today, and they are a diverse group and will get only more diverse. Progressive organizations understand that building truly inclusive cultures for all forms of visible and invisible human uniqueness allows them to create belonging and psychological safety, ultimately unlocking greater levels of creativity and human potential. Many organizations are now making progress in creating highly skilled leadership teams and boards that are more diverse and include 2SLGBTQ+ individuals.

Politically, we have been more advanced here in Canada. In 2017, Bill C-16 was passed, which was an amendment to the Canadian Human Rights Act and Criminal Code that added gender identity and gender expression as protected categories. This was a welcome step toward acceptance, but there was also the issue of conversion therapy, which was still legal in Canada in 2017 (it became illegal across all provinces in 2022). Conversion therapy started more than a century ago as a way to change people's sexual orientation or gender identity if they were not heterosexual or cis-gender. It attempted to repress sexual desire and gender identity, and over the course of 130 or so years, caused tremendous damage to the emotional well-being and lives of the 2SLGBTQ+ community. Conversion therapy has taken many forms, such as psychoanalysis, prayer healing, exorcism, talk therapy, aversion therapy (where gay men were punished for their desires), and testicular implants in gay men to boost testosterone. The idea that homosexuality is essentially a disease that can be cured shows up in Richard von Krafft-Ebing's 1886 work *Psychopathia Sexualis*, in which he recommends hypnosis as the solution. The view that homosexuality was a disorder remained intact in the medical world for almost a century. It wasn't until 1973 that homosexuality was removed from the *Diagnostic and Statistical Manual of Mental Disorders.*

In early July 2021, I sent an email to then Senator George Furey, asking him to take leadership to ensure Bill C-6 passed, making conversion therapy illegal in Canada. I told him I was a woman with gender-affirming experience and the parent of four children. "I have witnessed at all levels of my life the mental impact of judgement and rejection, overt lack of acceptance, and conversion attempts," I wrote. "These conversion attempts to 'take the gay out of the human' have been proven to be not only ineffective but very detrimental to mental health, [causing harm] including suicide... We cannot let this happen in Canada."

But for decades, we did let it happen. And this simply added to the pressing mental health burden borne by 2SLGBTQ+ youth. My concern with the delay of Bill C-6 was that it would cost lives. When I got in touch with Senator Furey, it was just before Parliament was scheduled to be recessed. And there was also the possibility of a fall election, which meant the bill could be delayed by several months. In those several months, how many would take their lives? One would be too many. I felt it was imperative that the bill be passed quickly—it was literally a matter of life and death. Luckily, Senator Furey agreed. Bill C-6 was passed in December 2021, making conversion therapy illegal in Canada. It was comforting that the vote in the House of Commons was unanimous, by all political parties and ministers. A proud moment for Canada.

In 2018, the Liberal government mandated that Statistics Canada reflect gender diversity in the national census. The 2022 census differentiated between "sex at birth" and "gender" for the first time, providing a snapshot of the transgender population. The transgender population in Canada was listed at 100,815, though both Statistics Canada and 2SLGBTQ+

advocates suggested that the actual population is much higher. Advocates would have preferred "sex assigned at birth" rather than "sex at birth" which still implies it's something that is read on the body.

Statistics Canada noted that the proportion of transgender and non-binary people was "three to seven times higher" for those born between 1981 and 2006 than for those born before 1981. This was viewed as a result of the younger generation's greater acceptance of non-binary people—they are more comfortable reporting their gender identity than older generations. The existing census isn't perfect, but it is a clear step in the right direction. It is a recognition of the transgender and non-binary community.

Many countries around the world have taken steps like Canada to protect the rights of all people, including sexual orientation and gender identity and expression. This is not the time to slide backward with restrictive laws. The mental health, emotional well-being, and productive lives of so many are at stake. It is the time to keep moving forward at the corporate level as well. A company's ability to attract and retain the best talent and unlock human potential relies on advancing mental health support, access to critical services, and building kinder and more inclusive organizations.

PUBERTY IS A PARTICULARLY challenging time for transgender people. Your body is undergoing dramatic changes. The masculine body fills out and grows hair, the voice gets deeper. For someone who is wired and identifies as female, I can tell you, this is an ongoing horror, watching your body go in the opposite direction of your heart and brain. I struggled with my male body parts. I have never liked body hair on myself and was horrified to see it sprout up in puberty.

As I mentioned, I grew up in an isolated community, in a world where media meant three television channels and two newspapers. Societal norms were reinforced by the media, in the church, and in the school system. Gender identity, back then, especially on a farm, was binary. It was very simple: You were male or female. Gender identity was a function of genitals and reinforced by social constructs. If you were a boy, you played with trucks; if you were a girl, you wore dresses and played with dolls. So, puberty was a particularly confusing and vulnerable time for me. It is a vulnerable time for anyone, but especially for 2SLGBTQ+ youth.

The explosion of media and the proliferation of information and social media means that everyone can find people like themselves; they can discover a community online. But social media is a double-edged sword. While 2SLGBTQ+ people can find education, solace, and friendship and understanding online, they can also stumble onto hatred and oppression, heightening fear, anxiety, and mental health challenges.

During COVID-19, everyone relied more heavily on social media for connections. We were wary of any in-person gathering, public or private. Sitting in our homes in front of our computer screens was the best way to keep in touch with friends. But the limitations of social media were laid bare. Rates of depression and anxiety skyrocketed. In 2019, there were 1.9 million interactions with Kids Help Phone. In 2021, the calls more than doubled. In 2019, 40 percent of texting conversations were with 2SLGBTQ+ youth; by 2022, that had risen to 55 percent.

The pandemic meant that most of us spent disproportionate time at home. Research has shown that 2SLGBTQ+ children and youth often face more rejection from their families than non-2SLGBTQ+ youth. Being stuck at home took a huge emotional toll on 2SLGBTQ+ youth. In the Canadian Trans Youth Health Survey, respondents reported better mental health when they felt cared for and supported by family. Outside of their home environment, many 2SLGBTQ+ youth feel they have to disguise their authentic self for their own safety. Only half live their felt gender 100 percent of the time. This creates yet more problems with dysphoria and mental health, and poor mental health is one of the reasons people avoid the health care system—it's a vicious circle.

In the transgender community, the highest rates of suicide, suicide attempts, and suicide ideation occur when gender dysphoria is experienced and when people are trying to access care and transition services, whether it's hormones or surgery. The wait can be years. This is the highest risk area for suicide, and one that can be changed. The process can be streamlined.

Dr. June Lam is a psychiatrist at CAMH. "There are not enough providers who prescribe hormones," he said to me in 2022. "Any family doctor, any nurse practitioner can prescribe hormones because it's already in their scope. Some doctors already prescribe hormones but many family doctors or nurse practitioners were never trained specifically to prescribe hormones for transgender people. They often feel it's outside of their scope, but it's not. Accessing hormones is incredibly difficult."

It is difficult even in Toronto, a city that has one of the largest 2SLGBTQ+ communities in the world. Accessing surgery is even more difficult. People may want to consult a psychologist or therapist to discuss their specific situation, and that can be a wait of a few months or longer. Then they see their family doctor. Family doctors don't always feel comfortable applying for government funding for surgeries like chest reconstruction surgery, but the applicant needs a physician or nurse practitioner to fill out a form for the Ministry of Health in Ontario that says they are eligible.

The wait to see someone like Dr. Lam is four to eight months. Sometimes, the first appointment is just talking, necessitating a second appointment and another wait time. They the person can apply for the funding, and the Ministry of Health can take up to four to six months to approve it. If the funding is approved, then the family doctor has to refer the person to a surgeon. The wait time at Women's College Hospital in Toronto, where a lot of the surgeries are done, is a year and a half to two years.

"From the time a transgender person figures out who they are," said Dr. Lam, "[and] what they want, then go to the family doctor, then they see me, then get a referral to the surgeon, then actually get surgery, the wait is often three to five years. And that's on the quick end of things. For some people it can be ten or even fifteen years."

For many gender-affirming surgeries, you need two people to refer you, two letters to apply for funding. Not everyone has a family doctor, and it can cost money for those who can't find people covered by health care.

Another hurdle is encountering transphobia in the health care system. Physicians and nurses sometimes use the wrong pronoun, or use the person's legal name instead of their chosen name. And getting a name change can be complicated. A physician has to write a letter saying they have assessed the person and agree with their change of sex designation on all forms of their government-issued ID. Without that official ID, it may not be possible to vote, resulting in further disenfranchisement.

A trans PULSE Ontario study showed that one of the most protective factors for mental health and suicidality is getting

We can solve complex
problems and work together
out of a place of shared
kindness, love, empathy, and
connection to ourselves,
each other, and nature.

———————————

your government ID changed. If a person can get at least one piece of government-issued ID that is consistent with their gender, their rate of suicide goes down dramatically.

The first part of my name-changing process was knowing I was wired Katherine on the inside. But to know is one thing, while having to present ID that represents your deadname, the name you were given versus the person you really are, is another thing. Imagine living fully as Katherine (or Monique or Angela, or whoever you are) and then having to present your credit or debit card or your passport with your deadname. It's an incredibly unnerving experience. You think, *Am I going to get pulled over by the police and harassed? Are people going to talk too loudly and question my ID in a public environment and out me? Are they going to mock me?*

There are all kinds of fears that go through a person's mind when they're living as their true self but without ID that reflects it. That fear of being outed, of being ridiculed or harassed, is very real.

To change your birth certificate, you must get government permission. For me, this happened quite seamlessly. It's important to note that my birth certificate says Katherine—one of the beautiful aspects of Canada is that your birth certificate can be changed to reflect your true name. It feels very affirming.

Next, you go to change your driver's licence and health card. I was scared that some rookie clerk would grill me and embarrass me in public. It did take a long time waiting in line and for them to process the paperwork. Yet the person was incredibly kind and understanding.

What I was most fearful of was my passport, because I was flying on a business trip the October after my coming out, and I had to get my passport updated quickly. I was at the passport office dropping off my new birth certificate, my driver's licence, the form, and my old passport. At the time, I was thinking, *The federal government is going to be the hardest of all.* Yet the man took my forms, and said, "Thanks very much. Can you come back in thirty minutes for your new passport?"

I said, "What?"

He said, "Yeah, no problem. Can you come back in thirty minutes for your new passport? We'll put you through the fast-track process."

It was beyond affirming!

We are living in an open and transparent world where information flows freely, beyond traditional social norms and constructs. We are experiencing overwhelming and unprecedented climate stress, economic stress, and social stress. We've proved we can use our intelligence and collaboration to fragment and divide and grow economically, often out of anxiety and fear.

Never before has it been more critical that we evolve into a way of human being—a way of being that centres on self-love as well as kindness, empathy, love, and deep understanding of each other, so we can work together to solve complex problems in the world we share.

8

Connectedness:
Duality and Non-Duality

Love is the recognition of oneness in the world of duality.

ECKHART TOLLE

FTER YEARS of making sense of myself and understanding how I am uniquely wired, I have found myself repeatedly tearing down the walls of biases I had built to fit into a world of extreme duality. This included living in a man's world, then a woman's world, with all the social conditioning and biases that accompany them. Every day, I find new biases I did not know I had.

Yet non-duality isn't new. In the seventeenth century, Sir Isaac Newton, mathematician, physicist, astronomer, and theologian, formulated the laws of motion and universal gravitation that influenced the dominant scientific viewpoint for centuries. This viewpoint fuelled our desire to break things down to the smallest element to understand nature and fuel innovation, progress, and growth. Newtonian science was superseded in the twentieth century by Einstein's theory of relativity. Einstein offered a more holistic model that embraced "all living creatures." Now we're in the era of quantum physics. Quantum science has the potential to transform our view of gravity and its connection to space and time. It is revealing how everything in the universe is connected to everything else in ways we are still coming to understand. And the ability to see and appreciate interconnection and relationships among all things holds the key to moving forward in new, more holistic and sustainable ways. In quantum mechanics, "wave-particle duality" describes matter having both wave-like and particle-like characteristics, an idea that clashes with classical physics theory. But duality is a natural part of our lives.

BY SEPTEMBER 2019, when I first returned to the office, I was living fully and physically as my true self. And work was amazing, with incredible impact and results being achieved. My fall was busy with town halls and business planning, but there were other changes occurring that were daunting. For one thing, Rosemary and I separated in October 2019; we both needed our space. There was only one child left at home, witnessing my new life every day. The three older kids were away at school, on their own journeys. As I said in the introduction, it takes millions of years to come to a single moment when a story plays out. What I didn't mention is how multiple stories can be playing out at one time. And that was my duality that fall.

I had made a successful segue in my career, but for the first time in my life, I found I was facing being alone and living alone. Most people go through some form of anxiety, sadness, or depression when they become empty nesters at mid-life. I experienced that as well as living in the world as Katherine—my true self—a woman, and a separation, and living alone.

I hadn't been very successful at living alone before. I had tried moving away from the farm when I went off to college and again when I started working at the bank—I moved out twice and then back home within two or three months both times. In spite of a challenging home environment, I had a bigger fear of being alone in the world, of being abandoned. And from 2019 to 2022, I was really dealing with my deeper childhood trauma of fear of abandonment. But that's also when my spiritual journey began to accelerate.

Most species are born with either male or female genitals to enable procreation. However, when these distinct dualities create bias and give way to more abstract forms, the picture becomes more challenging. Left brain versus right brain, leading to biases of less intelligent versus more intelligent, or more creative versus less creative. There are social dualities: white versus those of colour, heterosexual and cis-gender versus 2SLGBTQ+, "normal" versus neurodiverse, male versus female, masculine versus feminine traits. Each leads to biases—strong versus weak, dominant versus subservient, leader versus follower. These biases obscure the idea of human uniqueness and potential. What if, for a moment, we suspended all biases, and sat in awe of these extraordinary forms of uniqueness and beauty?

I was struck by this question when I watched the movie *Barbie*. Director Greta Gerwig shows us Barbie Land, where women are in control and men are secondary figures, lacking confidence and purpose. It was a reverse mirror of the real world, where men are traditionally in positions of control and women are in supporting roles or, worse, victims, subservient and objectified. But neither version works. All individuals have both masculine and feminine traits, the special blend of which makes them unique. Slotting people into gender and societal norms only prevents them from fully bringing their distinctive abilities to the world and creates stress, anxiety, and health issues.

Women and minority groups are still vastly under-represented. And these places of leadership—public institutions, government, corporate world—are missing out on a richness of perspective, ability, and potential that is needed now more than ever. Solving this should be easy, you might think, and yet bias, set ways of thinking, and risk aversion keep getting in the way.

COVID-19 created an opportunity for us to understand different attributes under crisis. Research showed that countries led by women had lower fatality rates. But the glass ceiling and glass cliff still exist, invisible barriers to advancement and sustainment of women at senior levels. Often, when women are finally given the chance to lead, it is during a crisis, when something is already not working and the odds of failure are high.

Yet when the *Harvard Business Review* looked at the overall leadership effectiveness ratings of men and woman, they noted that women perform better during a crisis. On thirteen of nineteen competencies (among them, Takes Initiative, Learning Agility, Inspires and Motivates, Develops Others, Builds Relationships, and Displays High Integrity and Honest Leading), women rated higher. The highest male rating was in Technical or Professional Expertise, where they scored a 55, only two points ahead of women. Women exceeded this 55-point male high on seventeen of nineteen competencies. Hampering the advancement of women and other under-represented groups is one of our most basic human failings, and it has hindered the progress of our modern hierarchy and society.

Having lived in a man's world and having spent more than thirty years in leadership roles has given me a unique perspective. I know many men who suppress aspects of their innate character and personality—often creative, interpersonal, and

COVID-19 created an opportunity for us to understand different attributes under crisis. Research showed that countries led by women had lower fatality rates.

———————————

softer skills—to fit into a male stereotype, an archetype. I did this to some extent as well. These men experience stress, sometimes extreme, in not being their authentic selves because of the pressure to be the male "hero," to be Hercules.

One of the things I learned during the InclusionDialogues sessions was that vulnerability can also be a strength—for both men and women. Once I knew who someone was and where their kindness, compassion, empathy, resilience, and determination came from, I had greater confidence in giving them new opportunities. I knew more about their gifts and what shaped them.

Today, we have more men and women in positions of influence and power who are shaking away biases and demonstrating real authenticity, awareness, insight, and sustained action. However, this progress isn't enough. Still, there are too many leaders suppressing parts of themselves out of fear and conditioning and not creating the environments in which they and others can flourish as whole human beings. The world is still missing out on the mix of skills, experiences, and perspective required to operate in a more thoughtful, holistic, and sustainable way.

FOR MANY, INCLUDING ME, the pandemic was hard. Being alone took getting used to. I started to research and practise meditation, and I went on a spiritual journey to figure out what I wanted to do with the next chapter of my life.

One beautiful thing that happened was that I had the privilege of spending time with writer and professor Betty Sue Flowers. She is also the former director of the Lyndon Baines Johnson Library and Museum and had a career as a veteran practitioner of scenario planning at Royal Dutch Shell. My life coach, Sally from New Zealand, recommended I read a book by Joseph Jaworski called *Synchronicity: The Inner Path of Leadership*. In the book, Jaworski related how he met Betty Sue Flowers, now a friend, through synchronicity, how he was drawn to her and reached out to her spontaneously to ask if she'd be open to talking to him. And to his surprise, she said yes.

In addition to being an author, Jaworski was a renowned strategy and leadership expert at Shell Global doing long-term strategic scenario planning. Global organizations need to develop points of view on the direction of the world to inform their strategic plans and business plans. Shell developed some of the most thoughtful and insightful scenarios in the world to support its business efforts. Together, Jaworski and Betty Sue further evolved this work to create different truly global scenarios based on biases, beliefs, and choices: scenarios that could divide and further hurt society and our planet, and choices that could move us toward connectedness and a more integrated, sustainable, and harmonious world. Betty Sue's work with Shell was informed by her deep understanding of stories and mythology.

I reached out to Betty Sue on LinkedIn, just as Jaworski did. I wrote to her, "I have no idea whether we're supposed to know each other or not. Yet I feel drawn to speak to you. There's something about you and the work that you've done with Joe that inspires me. I'm writing a book. Would you be open to talking to me?"

She said yes and we met on a one-hour Zoom call. She encouraged me in my writing and to continue on my spiritual journey. I was so taken in by her wisdom, peace, and presence. We discussed perspectives on leadership, society, and sustainability, the role of the world's largest organizations and governments, and the education system in building a truly sustainable world. She told me, "You hold a key to moving humanity from duality to non-duality, given your story and your life experiences."

Betty Sue recognized my journey and life experiences in both a man's world and a woman's world—my personal understanding of biases that inform how girls and boys are raised and conditioned—as a great gift. It was because of my interaction with her that I realized I needed to have an appreciation of my identity, gender, sexual orientation, and neurodiversity coupled with an understanding of the farm, and of large organizations and the business world. Everything was connected and has made me who I am today.

Betty Sue shared her perspective that humanity is shifting from a belief system founded on the idea that economic growth will create prosperity for all to a belief system that is inclusive and holistic, and centred on the health of the planet, the health of the individual, and the health of society. To do that, people need to understand and embrace non-duality. "What's emerging," she said, "is a new synthesis of science, spirituality, and leadership as different facets of a single way of being." In other words, a more conscious, connected, and integrated way of being.

In the 2011 book *Ancient Greece, Modern Psyche: Archetypes in the Making*, Betty Sue's chapter describes the myths of the male hero (Hercules) and female subordinate or victim, both of which date back to ancient Greece, about 2,500 years ago. She relates how these biases remain in our unconscious psyche and archetypes of today. She also explains how the Greek goddess Athena challenged this male hero/female victim myth by embodying a number of attributes that modern culture sees as contradictions. Athena was a beautiful young woman but also a fierce warrior and the goddess of wisdom. Traditional thinking dictates that if you're young, you can't be wise; if you're a warrior or tomboy, you aren't beautiful. And on top of all that, Athena was both a selfless nurturer and a strategic thinker and leader.

We need more Athenas. We are at a time when both men and women need to embrace and bring both their feminine and masculine traits to their life and work to generate the best and most holistic outcomes, and to be true to their natural essence and emotional well-being.

Masculine and feminine energies have nothing to do with being male or female. They are energies that are in each of us, both required to be in harmony. Feminine energy is holistic, interconnected, and circular, while masculine energy is linear and logical. Masculine energy is protective, while feminine energy is nurturing. Masculine energy is knowledge and doing, while feminine energy is a deeper knowing and being. Knowledge is static, and knowing is dynamic. Feminine energy can see the possibilities that are invisible to the structured, masculine energy. When people create from their feminine energy, they tap into their intuition, creative potential, and higher consciousness. Feminine energy does not suppress emotion. It means recognizing emotion as valuable messengers and insight. In our modern productive and systematic world, our true feminine energy has been suppressed, hurting us individually and globally.

It felt validating to finally be able to embrace my own feminine energy—my emotional, creative, and intellectual self. My ways of thinking, feeling, and being had always been different, but when I embraced them, they became a source of strength.

———

FOR ME, ONE OF THE GREATEST and potentially threatening science-driven innovations of our time is artificial intelligence (AI). AI is programmed by humans with inherent biases built into that original program or code. AI then learns, adjusts, and procreates quickly, at scale and over time. The consciousness and ethics humans build into AI has the potential to generate at scale and speed up positive or negative outcomes for our planet, society, and individual and collective well-being. We need to ensure the machines and objects we create are built to ensure health, well-being and sustainability for all, people and planet.

Here's an example from my own life of the human element needing to be part of the business plan. Following the 2008 financial crisis, I was in a CEO position leading a restructuring in the Caribbean where a bank was struggling. Employees knew it, yet it was not being talked about. My promise to employees was that I would do everything in my power to save the company and as many jobs as possible. It was not uncommon for me to be emotional and cry out of empathy for the fearful and anxious employees and their families. In some countries, the post-financial-crisis world had unemployment rates close to 30 percent. It was soul crushing.

Every decision we made was to save both the company and as many jobs as possible. We were careful to balance short-term performance, because it was about saving the bank now, with building something better and sustainable for the long term. It's now fifteen years later, and the company has achieved record performance because the mission and approach that were set in the beginning were carried on.

Similarly, front line employees in banking were worried about losing their jobs because of technology and mobile devices. My promise to them was to reinvent their jobs—to take them from being transactional to being advisory, so they could become teachers and advisors. In one job, in one area, we went from over ten thousand employees to less than five thousand in a handful of years. And we didn't issue terminations or departure packages because we managed by developing new skills and promoting people. In other areas, we added new jobs. The workforce was still more than twenty-five thousand at the end of eight years, and growing. What grew were more advisory and education-type roles. We invested in people with a view to the middle and longer term . . . a view to sustainability.

My belief was that if human beings leaned into what made them uniquely human, which were things like empathy, compassion, and contextual advice—not AI advice, but something that is deeper—we would be able to prove that people would continue to turn to human advisors to help them navigate their largest fears around money. Over the decade, we went on to achieve record client loyalty and business results while transforming what a workforce did.

It's about being human-centred and holistic, which gets into non-duality. We're not separate; we are all one. We're part of something bigger. We are connected. We're part of humanity and society and nature; there's an undeniable interrelationship. Quantum physicists will tell you that there's an energetic interrelationship that we all have and share, across everything.

When we work together compassionately with curiosity, kindness, a common mission—of a healthy planet, healthy society, self-love—inevitably, we solve problems. We end up coming up with more holistic and sustainable solutions as individuals.

For me, it's all about understanding our own humanity and interrelationship as humans within ourselves, with each other, and with nature and beyond. We need to consider what makes us similar, which is that we all want to belong; we all want love, joy, and peace.

Rose von Thater-Braan, organizer of an integrated learning centre that shares studies of Indigenous knowledge and science, has suggested that the difference between Indigenous

It's all about understanding
our own humanity… what makes
us similar, which is that we all
want to belong, and we all want
love, joy, and peace.

———————————

science and Western science starts with intent. The common purpose, or intent, that has driven Western science is to understand nature in order to better control or commodify it. With Indigenous science, the fundamental intent is to become more human and to learn how to live in harmony with nature and one another. Central to this happening is the transformation of our global education systems. As Nelson Mandela said, "Education is the most powerful weapon which you can use to change the world." Delphine Le Serre, a friend, physicist, PhD, and AI expert, is dedicating her life to building an education model for the future, a model that, along with science like AI, centres on human development. The founder of EdHu2050, she understands that science and innovation must be done in combination with the embrace of nature and true human uniqueness. It must be tied to unlocking and developing the best of human potential.

Also central to this thesis is leadership of the future. Together, science, humans' connectedness, embracing and unlocking our potential, and next-generation leadership at all levels are required to building sustainable organizations and societies for the future.

9

Building Sustainable Organizations and Societies

My job is to create a world that lasts two hours.
Your job is to create a world that lasts forever.
STEVEN SPIELBERG

ILL MARRIOTT, former CEO of the hotel chain that bears his name, once said, "We are asleep until something wakes us up." As far as climate change goes, many of us are still asleep. So much of it is happening offstage—the melting glaciers and subtle rises in sea levels. But in June 2023, smoke from Quebec wildfires blanketed Washington, DC, and New York, resulting in the worst recorded air quality in the world for that day. The dense, particulate-laden air affected everyone. The cities looked apocalyptic, cloaked in orange fog. I remember the orange sky in Toronto. It lasted a while. I also remember this gray and orangey hue in cottage country as well, north of Toronto. An air quality advisory was issued for 120 million Americans. Perhaps the only benefit to a catastrophe like this is that it certainly wakes us up.

Indigenous people have been awake for thousands of years. Many Indigenous leaders and cultures operate with a wisdom and consciousness about their society and the natural world. It guides them to make more holistic choices out of a deep respect for the earth, their community, and future generations. We can learn a lot from them.

In 1968, ecologist Garrett Hardin wrote an essay titled "The Tragedy of the Commons," in which he described how competing individual interests with access to a common resource can exploit it to the point at which it becomes exhausted and worthless. The concept wasn't new—it appears as early as Aristotle, but it was largely theoretical when Aristotle talked about it. There were abundant resources and few people in the world. Now we have the opposite situation.

Indigenous people have understood that humans are part of nature, rather than its landlord. Many Nations have been careful not to exploit resources that are key to their survival, such as buffalo, salmon, clean water. They have remained in harmony with nature rather than exploiting it for short-term gain. And now we are consulting with Indigenous leaders on how to steward our resources.

I was privileged to meet and work with Phil Fontaine, who was National Chief of the Assembly of First Nations (AFN) for three terms. I believe he's one of the most effective Indigenous leaders Canada has witnessed. We were both signatories on the Corporate Challenge Memorandum of Understanding, which was designed to accelerate partnerships between corporations and Indigenous people. It included a commitment to hiring and training Indigenous talent, procurement practices, and deployment of capital into Indigenous projects. Later, I had the privilege of hiring Phil into the company as a senior advisor on Indigenous issues.

It was under Phil's watch that the Indian Residential Schools Settlement Agreement was initiated, and national and papal apologies were achieved. In 1990, he publicly related his own traumatic experience at a residential school, the first such disclosure by a prominent Indigenous leader. The AFN is a complex constituency: over 630 First Nations that have many common interests but also diverging and sometimes competing ones. It is further complicated by the fact that the national chief then has to negotiate with federal and provincial governments, dealing with a host of grievances, some of which are more than a century old.

What were the leadership qualities that made Phil's tenure so effective? First of all, he visited his constituents, who were spread across the country, often in remote northern regions. "I travelled extensively across the country," he told me. "I went to just about every community in the country—small communities, large communities." His engagement also included civic, provincial, and federal government leaders. Phil engaged with all constituents, listening deeply and working to identify critical issues, and then formulated a plan that was understood by all. He facilitated an open dialogue that renowned physicist David Bohm concluded was required to move the world from its modern divided and fragmented approach to one of connectedness and shared sense of empathy and higher understanding. Through dialogue, Phil brought a level of clarity to an incredibly complex landscape.

Phil also possessed seemingly infinite patience and a sense of calm. But it turns out these were learned traits. "When I was younger," he said, "I was very aggressive and very angry. I didn't treat people nicely, especially government people. But then I learned at some point that it was counterproductive. So I changed my approach. I've been in terrific arguments with government ministers, but it was always behind closed doors. And when we emerged from behind those closed doors, it was two friends walking out."

Another quality of Phil's leadership that I identified with was humility. "I recognized that I wasn't the smartest guy in the room," he said. "Too often, I've seen leaders who want to demonstrate that they are the smartest in the room. I knew I wasn't, and I wasn't afraid to surround myself with very smart people."

Phil assembled a very talented team that was able to put together the historic Indian Residential Schools Settlement Agreement in 2007. "At one point, there were eighty lawyers around the table," he said, "so we had to be nimble. We based our approach on traditional Indigenous law."

The results of Phil's leadership were some of the most historic gains for Indigenous people in more than a century. There was an apology from the House of Commons and a private audience with Pope Benedict XVI. Hundreds of millions of dollars in reparations were distributed.

He has worked diligently to reverse decades-old policies that have undermined Indigenous progress, and to get Indigenous people in roles of corporate and academic leadership. "I think we can learn from each other," he said. "Indigenous peoples will bring a unique perspective to major corporations." Indigenous people can bring to organizations wisdom and sustainable practices that have served their cultures for centuries.

WE CAN LOOK AT how we lead through two lenses: human rights and human potential. On a human rights level, we can be guided by the United Nations' Universal Declaration of Human Rights, particularly Article 1: "All humans are born free and equal in dignity and rights." This is one of the most powerful passages I have ever read. At the Canadian Museum for Human Rights in Winnipeg, the quote is displayed as a centrepiece. The museum tells countless stories of human atrocities, lest we forget the evil humankind is capable of, but it also tells stories of human courage and hope, so we can be inspired by the good we are capable of.

Earlier in my career, from 2005 to 2009, I was the bank president of the Prairies region, living in Winnipeg. That's when the Museum for Human Rights was being birthed. Israel "Izzy" Asper, who was a prominent Canadian, had had this vision to build the first museum dedicated to human rights that would exist outside of the nation's capital. Six months after the announcement of the museum, Asper passed away, and his daughter Gail picked up the mission.

I developed a real passion for the museum and its purpose of telling the stories of human atrocities that had occurred in Canada and around the world, whether against Indigenous peoples, Jewish people, or anyone who has faced serious hurt and discrimination. I helped the museum do some fundraising, and my family and I became donors. Later, when I came out, the museum asked me to be their keynote speaker. It was during COVID-19, so it was a virtual gala. I told my story and my leadership and life lessons to the three thousand people in attendance. And then the following year, in 2021, I went back to Winnipeg and did another talk with an intimate audience, this time in person.

The Canadian Museum for Human Rights building is designed with floors that spiral up to a shaft of light—love and light—at the top. Alabaster lines the walkways in the museum, and ascending them, you eventually end up in a very bright glass room, in the Israel Asper Tower of Hope. When I visit the museum, I take the elevator to the top floor, to the place of hope, love, and light, first. And then I work my way down to the main floor, where it's darkest. I think this approach mirrors my natural wiring—to go out to a place in the future where there is love, hope, and clarity, and then come back to the challenges of today. The place where leadership must be better and the work can be and needs to be done.

I remember the day in 2021 when I went to do the talk. I went up the elevator with my friends Joe and Andreas. Reading the first article from the Universal Declaration of Human Rights, I cried. "All humans are born free and equal in dignity and rights." All I could think was, *It's not so hard. Like, how hard is it for any human being to understand that?* I started my talk that day with that simple message.

I started to cry as I gave my talk, and I said, "Why is it that we as human beings find it so hard to understand that we're all born innocent and free and deserving of dignity and love and respect? That nature, plants, and animals deserve the same?" I believe moments like these are a reminder that a leader needs to be reflective, to be on a deeper discovery and way of being journey.

About leadership, Einstein is often attributed for saying, "The leader is the one who, out of the clutter, brings simplicity... out of discord, harmony... and out of difficulty, opportunity." We can do this when we take time to really be reflective, to really give ourselves the room to feel deeply, and to create space to heal within ourselves.

Recognizing, healing, and unlocking human potential is both art and science. Over the longer term, it is fundamental to the health of any organization or society, and fundamental to the health of our planet.

An example of failing to recognize potential may be in Tom Brady's story. Brady is a former National Football League quarterback, widely considered the greatest football player of all time. He is the winner of a record seven Super Bowls and holds more than a dozen NFL records. Yet he was the 199th

Moments like these are
a reminder that a leader
needs to be reflective, to be
on a deeper discovery and
way of being journey.

———————————————

player drafted. The NFL is the richest sports league in North America and employs hundreds of people to monitor players as young as twelve, trying to gauge their future potential. How is it that all of them failed to see Brady's potential?

I relate to his story because my own potential was missed by my early teachers—who were themselves taught to teach one way within a mechanized system—but then seen by my friend's father, who insisted I try banking. The system believed I was troublesome because I was inquisitive, creative, sensitive, and playful. Meanwhile, my friend's father saw a leader.

Problematically, we often measure people by standardized metrics and systems the industry has always used. Brady didn't look particularly athletic. He was tall and lanky and vulnerable-looking. And he was slow. Speed is measured by 40-yard sprints, and Brady's time remains one of the slowest for a quarterback. So, by that metric, he wasn't an attractive prospect. But the skills he possessed were more difficult to measure. He had an uncanny ability to see the entire field in little more than a second. This allowed him to get rid of the ball quicker than any other quarterback, and it also effectively made up for his lack of speed. But it is difficult to measure vision. It was also impossible to predict his longevity. The average NFL career is 3.3 years; Brady played for twenty-three seasons, from 2000 to 2022. And finally, the scouts had no way to measure his passion to win, his deep conviction. He was soft-spoken but possessed the competitive fire seen in elite athletes like Serena Williams, Wayne Gretzky, and Michael Jordan. Had they looked at Brady through a different lens, the scouts may have ranked him much higher.

To be fair, it isn't always easy to gauge someone's potential, but the more we know about that person, the greater our chance to see that potential. A prospective hire may have an MBA from a prestigious business school, and while that's a welcome asset, it's no guarantee of future success. Another candidate may not have a degree but could have unseen qualities that will be of great benefit in the future. This was certainly my own story, with my four-year high school diploma and two-year college diploma, and it has made me very aware of recognizing potential that others might not see. The human lesson stories of Mary, Susan, Robert, and Marieke all exemplify this message.

I remember seeing potential in a gentleman I worked with. In his leadership review, it came up that he had trouble making difficult decisions. He would not give up on a problem or on others. So, just as with the InclusionDialogues, I asked the question, "Where does that come from?"

He told me about a tragedy from his childhood, and it was clear to me that he was someone who didn't want to leave anyone behind or let anyone down. Because I understood him better after that, I could really see his potential and knew to trust his process and instincts. I got to observe him diving to the bottom of a swimming pool, metaphorically speaking, to solve a problem with his team. Sometimes, I'd wonder if he was ever going to surface. Every time, sometimes three or maybe six months later, he would rise out of the water with his team and a box with a bow on it, perfectly tied. It was like he was holding his breath, solving problems down there with his team, so determined.

My job was to create psychological safety for him so he could be more efficient. Because he *would* solve it—just in a different way from you or me. This individual went on to have a profound impact in every job he had.

The high-potential individuals you promote bring their collective skills and experiences to senior executive roles. And they ultimately bring their values and behaviours, which shape your organization's values and culture. So you need to hire, then develop, individuals from a broad spectrum. If everyone has a similar background and went to the same university, then you likely won't get diverse perspectives. Leaders and organizations will miss out on the richness that comes with uncovering and embracing the dimensions of human uniqueness.

And we need diverse perspectives and societies where everyone can flourish. As the global population eventually declines, opportunities for economic growth will be reduced, with the remaining opportunity being to build inclusive societies and communities that thrive. In Canada, everyone's market and corporate client base is diverse. The choice of customers a business pursues reflects the same tendency as talent biases, informed by bias and missing the full potential of an individual or group. Canada is one of the most diverse countries in the world, and every developed country will only increase in all aspects of diversity. Counter to some of the immediate tensions around immigration or 2SLGBTQ+ populations, increasing diversity is an unstoppable force. The greater the grasp of those different cultures and backgrounds, the greater the chance for success.

I define diversity as "visible and invisible dimensions of human uniqueness." Visible aspects could be colour, race, assigned sex at birth, expressed gender, a disability. Invisible aspects could be lived traumatic experiences, work and life experiences, cultural history and experiences, neurodiversity, sexual orientation, or mental health challenges. The truth is that each of these represents many dimensions within all of us. They represent intersectionalities that make us the unique and beautiful individuals we are.

In non-dyslexic people, when they are asked a question, a specific region of their brain is activated to get the answer. But often in a dyslexic person, the whole brain lights up. So when I'm asked a question, my whole mind lights up. I have an episodic mind and spatial reasoning. I see stories and experiences, and I see the whole world, and then look for patterns and options to solve the problems. And that's how I problem solve. The book *The Dyslexic Advantage* by Brock and Fernette Eide unlocks the hidden gifts and potential of the dyslexic brain.

My mind remembers stories. It stacks up and looks at multiple stories quickly, then narrows down to what matters, to the issue or the answer. So I go out into the whole, to the future, and I picture what the future can be. Whether it's looking at life as Katherine or at a holistic business vision and strategy. And then I come back to today and I start building and manifesting the vision in a passionate and focused way with this very clear picture. My mind helps me see the whole and my heart and soul guide me to a place that feels just and right. Once I feel into something and connect the dots on it in the future, I can only move toward it holistically.

Part of the journey of affirming your gender is to tiptoe your way into it and see what it feels like. While I did this, I also pieced the puzzle together of what would life look like if I were Katherine. And then, wow, look out. I knew at that moment that I couldn't live in between: I had to be Katherine.

This might also be one of the things that really helped me in leadership—being guided by an inner knowing and compass, and the ability to sort information quickly and get to the point while also looking ahead. Now that I'm a CEO, so much of my role is holding empathy and space for employees, clients, society, and beyond; seeing the future; looking around corners, watching and mitigating shifts; and envisioning and re-envisioning how all the pieces fit together over time. That's how my mind is built. Approximately 25 percent of CEOs are dyslexic. Thirty percent of dyslexic people have ADHD. People think ADHD means you're just distracted. One of the greatest gifts of many ADHD people is that if they are engaged, they can become hyperfocused and lose themselves in their mission.

For years, I felt like I was broken because I didn't think and work in a traditional, masculine, linear, logical, methodical way. But the picture of the future and the pieces to get there were often clear to me. This type of long-term and holistic thinking did help me in coming out, and it has helped in business.

So we need a safe environment for people to voice their perspectives, because we all experience, see, and think differently. If people are afraid to be creative and suggest ideas, the company and society loses out on that potential. Psychological safety and belonging, inclusivity, is at the core of human leadership and unlocking human potential. It is up to leaders to create that environment where everyone is free to speak, to contribute. And leaders can't wait for contributions; they need to work with their team members and draw their creativity out of them in a way that promotes psychological safety. We are reluctant to share our views for all kinds of reasons: we don't think we're smart enough; we have an accent; we're too junior; we're too old; we're afraid to go against corporate or organizational norms. The leader has to get past this and create an environment focused on a higher sense of purpose, one that creates a sense of belonging and pulls everyone into the dialogue.

To do this, leaders have to know who they are leading, and not just the bare facts, like where they grew up, what their stated ambitions were during the job interview, and so on. The better we understand our employees and colleagues, the greater benefit to the organization. A person's lived experiences and vulnerabilities are a valuable asset, but to discover what those vulnerabilities are, leaders themselves need to show genuine openness, trust, and vulnerability. Leadership can set a tone of real understanding or a tone of concealment. Only the former is beneficial for the organization.

It is one thing to hire with diversity in mind. It is another to realize that potential. My former colleague James told me, "I think that most of the organizations that embrace diversity and inclusion aspire to do the right thing, but then they discover that inclusion is hard work, not something you switch on and off during heritage celebrations, whether it's Asian Heritage Month or Indigenous History Month or Black History Month or whatever." James has had a long, credible career in financial services as a senior leader and a highly respected community builder throughout his life. He said, "If inclusion is to work, leaders must lead by example. They have to initiate those experiences so that people do have a sense of belonging. Inclusion and equity are where the work is. It is often convenient, because of short-term economic priorities to deprioritize diversity and inclusion. But to the extent that you deprioritize diversity and inclusion, you're actually leaving growth and innovation opportunities on the table. You're leaving profit on the table. You're leaving shareholder value on the table."

Inclusion practices cannot be performative. They need to be part of how we lead and live all day, every day, part of our values and psyche. Diversity is a fact; inclusion is a choice.

A leader's role is to instill deep trust and confidence in their team. And where does confidence come from? It can come from achieving success, whether large or small. But success rarely comes without risk. Risk is the input; confidence, the outcome. And while success is the goal, failure is not the enemy. In his book, *Creativity, Inc: Overcoming the Unseen Forces That Stand in the Way of True Inspiration,* Ed Catmull, who served as co-founder of Pixar and president of Walt Disney Animation

Studios, wrote, "Failure isn't a necessary evil. In fact, it isn't an evil at all. It is a necessary consequence of doing something new." Every time we take a risk, there is the possibility of failure. But if we stay inside our comfort zone, we don't learn and progress, and we never find out what our own potential is. The same holds true for organizations, corporations, and societies.

Building an environmentally and socially sustainable world will take a lot of people out of their comfort zone. It will be filled with false starts and failures. But our lack of action risks creating a society that is outside everyone's comfort zone, defined by existential crisis and devastation.

———

TRUE SUSTAINABILITY exists when individuals, society, organizations, and our planet as a whole are in harmony and share common goals, today and in the future.

Short-term economic interests are necessary for any publicly traded company and economy, but they shouldn't overshadow middle- and long-term strategy. To lead an organization of any kind, it helps to think across three pillars: why the organization exists and what it wants to be (its higher purpose, vision, values, and strategy); the holistic outcomes it produces, including all environmental, social, and governance (ESG) metrics; and how it operates (its practices and the identification and deployment of financial and human resources). In each of these pillars, it is important to constantly adjust for the short-, middle-, and longer-term needs, strategic choices, and higher purpose of the organization.

In today's hyper-demanding world, so much attention is on the short term—the next quarter or the immediate year. The pressure of publicly traded companies to generate impressive quarterly results at the expense of long-term goals is one of the forces working against sustainability. These demands are often dictated by the economic forces at play beyond the organization itself. They are all part of a system that has been built over many decades, one that needs to change soon and quickly. It takes major foresight and courage for leaders to step out of the system and play the long game.

In many companies, five years is the distant future. In politics, it's an eternity. However, this is changing quickly. Increasingly, capital markets and investors are demanding transparency in organizations' impacts and progress with all stakeholders. ESG standards and measures, like the ones from the World Economic Forum, are beginning to taking hold. In time, I believe these will move from being performative, where firms pick their favourite metrics, to becoming consistent and transparent standards that will be audited like accounting and financial reporting standards are today. Some call this stakeholder capitalism. It is here to stay and will demand much more from both organizations and leaders. It's a critical piece in building the transparency, purpose, and responsibility required for the future.

In government, the first year of many political mandates is spent cataloguing the "mess" left behind by the previous administration. The last year (or in the case of the United States, the last two years) is essentially spent campaigning for the next election. Which leaves little time for policy and solving problems. Not a recipe for productivity, vision, or meaningful action. The payoff for some policies is too far away, so there isn't the same focus on what can be achieved in the near term. It can even be a disincentive, as something that takes five or ten years to accomplish could come to fruition under a new government. As others have noted, the reason it is so hard to initiate effective

climate policy is that the risks are immediate and the benefits are far in the future. While these dynamics are real, good
government policy is essential to building a more sustainable
planet and society. We see positive examples of this happening
in Europe, in Scandinavian countries.

The focus on short-term goals at the expense of longer-
term change is bolstered by the fact that the average tenure
of a Fortune 500 company CEO is four years. The new CEO is
understandably under pressure to deliver short-term results.
The market is a powerful and important force. "The market
is always right" is a popular dictum, and perhaps, in the final
analysis, that's true. But there is no final analysis. The market
is a continuum. And while it's necessary to produce short-term
results to satisfy shareholders today, there needs to be a much
greater and more holistic emphasis on the middle- and long-
term results across all stakeholders.

The essential, and challenging, argument here is between
traders and builders. The trader exists in the short term; the
builder looks to the long term. You need to be able to navigate
and withstand short-term pressures to build something special
and of value. Staying the course takes patience, thoughtfulness,
and courage, but if we ignore the long term in order to make
short-term gains, there might not be a long term. We need to
see and plan for what our organization will look like in five
years, in ten years. What will it look like in a truly environmentally and socially sustainable world?

The key to moving toward sustainability and sustainable
management practices rests primarily in the fourth pillar:
higher-purpose-driven, inclusive, and sustainable leadership,
culture, and talent. Leaders will require new skills to create,
guide, manage, and lead sustainable organizations. I define
this as SQ, or the sustainability quotient.

The sustainability quotient is a level of human and leadership consciousness that considers and accommodates all stakeholders. It requires self-awareness to challenge one's own biases. It incorporates humility, courage, wisdom, and the curiosity to look beyond how things are to how they could be more sustainable. It requires leaders to lead in generative and co-creative ways with a higher purpose and a sense of empathy and understanding at the core. These leaders will understand that each person's sense of obligation and responsibility to themselves, others, nature, and the planet is far more powerful than traditional hierarchy, control, and accountability. These are leaders who understand the potential and power of the systems and rhythms of nature. The next generation craves leaders who are vulnerable, curious, caring, kind, courageous, and holistic in their systems thinking. They crave leaders with greater consciousness. Leaders with SQ.

Are there alternative and evolved models of leadership, democracy, hierarchy, or market-based economies available to us? Yes, if we put our collective hearts and minds to it and study nature and naturally occurring systems and relationships. In the 2013 book *Braiding Sweetgrass*, Robin Wall Kimmerer describes a market of fresh and wholesome food where the only currency of exchange is gratitude, and the gratitude and appreciation results in sharing and no one taking more than they need. We need to keep asking deeper questions and pursuing new ways of leadership. We need to adapt and evolve now, in five years, and in ten years, in order to meet the conditions scientists tell us are required for the well-being of humanity and health of our home, Earth.

Sustainable corporate leadership is the single most important weapon against climate change. My friend John Izzo, a recognized author and expert in purpose- and empathy-driven

The next generation
craves leaders who
are vulnerable, curious,
caring, kind, courageous,
and holistic in their
systems thinking.

———————————

leadership, broke down four dimensions in the global fight for sustainability when I interviewed him in 2023. "Government really sets the table," he said, "but governments, especially in democracies, are inherently slow and inherently beholden to a variety of short-term interests to get elected. Individuals are very important because individual change, aggregately, has a huge influence on issues, whether it's climate or inclusion or racial justice or bullying. Then there's civil society, the non-profit sector, which I think is increasingly important in terms of impacting the business community; you see strange bedfellows now—Greenpeace working with Exxon, for example."

He continued, "But finally, I think that business is the most innovative, pervasive, and flexible part of the system. Business crosses all borders, especially large businesses. Business can turn on a dime on the decision of one person or a few people and go in a different direction. And business is used to innovating and investing in innovation and change. So for that reason, I think business is the most leverageable part of the system because of its capacity to move quickly, cross borders, and innovate."

With business as the single most powerful agent for sustainability, leadership has never been more important. "Good CEOs can do almost anything they want for a meaningful period of time if they can prove it works," John said.

And do we have good CEOs? Yes and no. We have made progress, but we need to make much more progress, and time is running out.

"I think organizations talk a good game," John said, "but at the end of the day, the shareholder and short-term interests are still in the driver's seat. It varies almost always based on the CEO and the senior leaders' commitment to doing something more profound. They need courage, because there are a lot of crosswinds."

Some of those crosswinds are political, as in the case of Disney not backing down on its support for 2SLGBTQ+ rights in the face of attacks from Florida's governor. And some are economic, such as the constant pressure for quarterly results.

But courage can pay dividends, both social and economic. A case in point is Nike with their ads featuring football quarterback Colin Kaepernick. In 2016, Kaepernick was the first NFL player to kneel during the playing of the national anthem to protest police brutality and racial inequality. It became a movement, and Kaepernick became a lightning rod, praised for his courage by supporters and labelled unpatriotic by critics. Nike's choice of Kaepernick as a spokesperson was controversial and received much blowback. But in the wake of that blowback, Nike sales soared.

"To use a Canadian analogy," John said, "Nike knew where the puck was going. They said their primary customers care more about inclusion and people being able to express themselves than they do about whether you kneel or don't kneel for the national anthem."

And where is the puck going now? Studies show that half of millennials and Gen Z regularly have anxiety about climate change. "Seventy percent of them take action every month to do something to impact climate change," John said. "So if you're a CEO, you say, What side of that issue do I want to be on? And not just the right side of history, but the right side of being smart as a business person. Hopefully, the system will start to choose CEOs who have that perspective because it's good for business, because it's aligned with where the puck is going in terms of younger people. But I also believe people can come to it through an epiphany. They can have their 'road to Damascus' moment. I do think all change is ultimately personal."

Jack Mezirow's *Transformative Dimensions of Adult Learning* is about the ideas of transformational learning and perspective transformation. Mezirow describes how our assumptions, or biases, become our frames of reference; they define and shape our individual perceptions, thoughts, and feelings, and determine what we think, feel, and do. Mezirow demonstrates how "disorienting dilemmas," or unexpected incidents or events in our lives, when thoughtfully examined, have the potential to show us we are not perceiving and understanding reality in accurate ways. Those who have experienced disorienting dilemmas in their life have a gift, a unique ability to challenge and change their biases and beliefs, to empathize, show compassion, learn, and grow.

Leaders of the future will need to be able to suspend and challenge their own, and their organization's, biases, beliefs, and models in order to move toward true sustainability. We need leadership that has vision: to see what the future holds, what the future could be, and the tools to get there.

The way I see it, sustainability isn't just about climate or the environment; it is also about social and economic sustainability shrinking the gap between the haves and the have-nots. As global populations shrink, governments and businesses will learn that new markets will come from within smaller populations, driving the need to create greater social and economic inclusivity for all.

There are role models who are making strides to balance the world of today while building for a new world. I had the unique privilege of spending time with Best Buy CEO Corie Barry during COVID-19. I was a member of World 50, an executive peer coaching organization, and attended its forum focused on the subject of planning the next chapter of your life.

Barry spoke about her experience as a woman in senior leadership roles. We were discussing the demanding trade-offs and pressures being faced by leaders and corporations—pressures to care for and support clients, communities, and employees while also pivoting business models and managing intense financial challenges. I asked her how she kept her energy up and her purpose alive. Her reply was, "Little notes." By that, she meant notes of appreciation received from customers, and from employees who work in warehouses or from home whose jobs she helped keep safe.

It's not by accident that Barry is the CEO of Best Buy. She succeeded another purpose-driven and inclusive leader, Hubert Joly, author of the book *The Heart of Business: Leadership Principles for the Next Era of Capitalism*. Both Barry and Joly are regarded as truly authentic and driven by a noble purpose.

In his book, Joly speaks clearly about the myths of leadership—that leaders are superheroes, that people are born leaders, that you cannot change. He writes about how he was once a top-down manager driven by data and analytics, and how he changed to focus on purpose and human magic. His leadership model became: Be clear about purpose, including your own, that of those around you, and the organization's. Be clear about your role as a leader. Be clear about who you serve. Be driven by values.

There are other leaders out there who are helping the complex transitions that lie ahead. In August 2022, Jennifer Rumsey became CEO of Cummins Inc., a global leader in engine manufacturing. Her strategy centres on energy transition, the pursuit of a zero-emissions future, and a culture of inclusivity, innovation, and learning. She is spearheading a revolution and partnering and investing with others to co-create and generate breakthrough solutions.

On January 15, 2014, Mary Barra became the first female CEO of a major automaker. She had been setting herself apart from other leaders since the age of eighteen, moving through roles like quality inspector to director of Human Resources. She developed a set of unique experiences and skills and knew the workings of General Motors, its opportunities and challenges. Her higher purpose is simple: zero crashes, zero emissions, zero congestion. She shares these goals with her team and is investing heavily in research and development, including electric vehicles and autonomous vehicles that communicate with other vehicles to avoid accidents and congestion.

Who is Barra as a leader? She is focused on empowering her workforce to make smart decisions, take calculated risks, and use their own judgement. She shows humility and responsibility in the most challenging and tragic of circumstances, and courage and compassion in protecting and advancing others. She sees her role as CEO as being in service of her employees, customers, communities, and the world.

From my perspective, Barry, Rumsey, and Barra are modern-day Athenas embracing all of their uniqueness and abilities, and leading toward a sustainable world.

––––––––––

THE GREATEST HONOUR of my career was receiving a Catalyst Honours Business Leaders Award in 2022, presented to a senior business leader for their work in the area of diversity, equity, and inclusion. It represented the impactful work done by more than twenty-five thousand colleagues and my leadership team. The award recognized that 58 percent of our senior executive roles were now occupied by women, up from 30 percent five years earlier. There were material improvements in the representation of BIPOC executives, and overall 2SLGBTQ+ representation doubled. It also recognized leading and differentiated inclusivity (psychological safety and belonging) results achieved across the vast swath of employees. Together my team and organization of diverse, purpose-driven, and inclusive individuals achieved record and leading customer and business results.

The Catalyst Honours award representative acknowledged me by saying, "Katherine Dudtschak embodies inclusion in every aspect of her professional and personal life. Through the sponsorship and development of formal initiatives, day-to-day dialogue with employees and leaders, and a transparent and inclusive leadership style, Katie promotes inclusion, diversity, and equity in a way that is both intentional and intuitive."

I was thrilled! It was better than just a good report card. It was acknowledgement at the highest level for my team and me. The nomination process considered that our senior management team had unanimously supported the introduction of required learning of Canadian Indigenous history and culture for all twenty-five thousand-plus advisors. The 4 Seasons of Reconciliation was an interactive, nine-module program that provided a basic foundation on the relationship between Canada and Indigenous peoples, covering topics such as residential schools, the history of treaties, Indigenous culture, and more.

I had also sponsored an external study involving American and Canadian C-suite leaders, focused on how gender norms and workplace culture have evolved in a post-#MeToo era (with the findings released in early 2022), and that was taken into consideration too.

At the ceremony, my speech began, "Diversity is a fact. Inclusion is a choice."

I deeply believe that. To create a truly inclusive world, you must embrace diversity at all levels. Take time to learn, develop

I define diversity as "visible and invisible dimensions of human uniqueness."

———————————

knowledge and awareness, challenge and change biases, and develop a shared sense of empathy for different human experiences. It's about being kind and curious about the world and the people around you.

COVID-19 affected most of the world. While we were all in it together, it wasn't a unifying force. Divisions deepened in those years. In Canada, we kept getting more grim news about the horrors of the residential school system and the toll it took on Indigenous people. Mass graves were discovered, retraumatizing survivors and causing grief and outrage. In the United States, the death of George Floyd and the Black Lives Matter movement underlined the systemic racism that existed in law enforcement and elsewhere. There was anti-Asian racism that stemmed from COVID, and anti-Muslim rhetoric.

As I detailed earlier, to deal with these divisions, we initiated leadership dialogues—storytelling and empathy experiences for senior executives and managers. They were stories never shared in the workplace before. Stories that ultimately built a much deeper level of empathy, care, compassion, and understanding of others and where their gifts and skills come from. This was then passed on to clients and communities, to society.

The Catalyst Honours award was an embodiment of what we'd all been through and what we'd learned. It marked the end of that chapter of my life. I will take those insights and principles with me to the next chapter, but there is a need continue to learn and to do more, much more.

THERE HAS NEVER BEEN greater pressure on society and organizations to become economically, socially, and environmentally sustainable. Corporate culture is inherently conservative, and many companies are focused on the present rather than embracing and anticipating the future. But the future is arriving at a faster pace than most of us anticipated, bringing with it both good and bad news. We need to adapt, and to do so quickly.

My thirty-plus years in banking gave me a sense of purpose, a deep calling to make a positive difference in the lives of colleagues, clients, society, and beyond. A desire to be of service.

From a naive farm kid, I grew into a leader responsible for more than twenty-five thousand colleagues and fifteen million clients in Canada. I've lived and worked in twelve different Canadian communities. I was given the responsibility of leading and saving a bank and thousands of jobs in nineteen Caribbean countries. I learned to lead in a more holistic and enduring, purpose-driven, and inclusive way.

I have made many mistakes over my life and career, and have learned many lessons about business, leadership, people, and the world. All of this gave me humility, and during my personal transformation, it gave me love and support. It was incredibly difficult to leave my work family in 2022, but I realized I needed time to rest, heal, reflect, and regroup in my own life, personally and professionally. With my family, friends, and colleagues, I had successfully navigated the journey of *becoming* Katherine. Now it was time for my inner journey and *being* Katherine.

I was conflicted. I wanted to stay close to the people at work who had supported and embraced me, but at the same time, I wanted to start a new chapter of my career as Katie, as Katherine. I wanted to take all I knew about life, leadership, and business and apply it to another endeavour, another chapter of my life and career. I wanted to take my authentic self into the world to do what I love and be of service.

A New Beginning

Beginning

Two Lives, One Lifetime

10

Katherine.

No one will come and save you. No one will come riding
on a white horse and take all your worries away.
You have to save yourself, little by little, day by day.
CHARLOTTE ERIKSSON

I N NOVEMBER 2022, I announced to my colleagues that I
was leaving the bank after more than thirty years. It was a
very emotional decision. My thousands of colleagues had
been my extended family, had supported me through my transformation, had embraced me with an outpouring of care and
love. But I had known for some time that I needed to start a new
chapter of my career. Despite the thousands of emails I received
from colleagues, I knew I needed to make a fresh start as Katie,
as Katherine.

I wanted the opportunity to take everything I knew as a
leader, business person, and human being, and bring it into the
future. To meet and work with others where they are at, for them
to meet me where I am at, and together go forward, be of service
and part of leading and building something special. My fresh
start wasn't about getting rid of my past, but rather integrating
and bringing my complete self into the future. I have no regrets

about the first half of my life, my incredible family and friends, the career I had, and the many experiences that shaped me.

But first, I needed some time to contemplate what the next step would look like. I had spent more than thirty years working hard, obsessively at times. My children were grown and I was now single. It was time to stop and take a look at both myself and the world. Little did I know that this much-needed break would bring about another hard and profound level of reflection, awareness, and growth.

I admit that fear of abandonment and loneliness spiked again when I left the bank. I was living alone, single, with grown kids and very few hobbies, given how I poured myself into my career and family. I was now choosing another chapter in my life and career, fearing that I wouldn't get a job, that nobody would want to hire a woman like me. It was a period filled with a new level of loneliness, grief, and fear, and it pushed me over the line toward a deeper level of spirituality. I set several intentions for this next chapter of life and eventually truly surrendered, and said, *I give up. Universe, show me the way.*

I decided to start by going to the most remote place on the planet. In early 2023, my eldest daughter and I took the trip of a lifetime to Antarctica. There are few places in the world where you can see nature at both its most pristine and its most vulnerable. Antarctica is home to the vast majority of Earth's ice and fresh water. It is the size of Canada and India combined. If all the ice of Antarctica melted, sea levels could rise as much as seventy metres, flooding large parts of the world.

The trip came about in an odd way. Like so many others during COVID, I worked from home. It was the most isolated I'd ever been. I was a year into my separation from Rosemary, without family and my work family. Growing up in a large family and always being in the workforce, I had never been alone before in my life. It wasn't something I was good at. Working from home, most of my connections were through Zoom or social media. On LinkedIn, I connected with Marieke, from the Netherlands, who did life coaching for women. As told earlier, she became part of the InclusionDialogues. We shared our stories, then developed an immediate friendship. I discovered that she had escaped an abusive relationship, finding the courage to leave with just a backpack and travel the world alone.

Because of her, I started doing weekend trips. I went to Quebec City and Niagara-on-the-Lake. I went hiking. I started pushing myself to get out into the world because I knew I needed to face my fears. I was living fully as Katherine.

In addition to life coaching, Marieke ended up in Australia working for a cruise line that did expeditions to Antarctica. I had the time, so I booked the trip. Marieke was going to be the guide, and I felt comfortable because I already knew her. But then COVID happened and the trip was postponed. By the time I went, Marieke was no longer leading that expedition—she had been promoted to coach other expedition leaders.

I chose Antarctica partly because I wanted to push myself to go on adventures, and this certainly qualified as an adventure. But I also wanted to see the most remote part of the planet. I had planned to go on my own, but it turned out that booking for two wasn't much more expensive than one, so I bought a ticket for my daughter. It was an amazing bonding experience for us. We flew first to Santiago, then Punta Arenas in Chile, and then to a military base on King George Island, the largest of the South Shetland Islands off the coast of Antarctica.

My daughter was twenty-four at the time. It was also amazing seeing it through her eyes. I'd never travelled with her as an adult. And to watch her interacting with other adults and being so curious, so kind, and so present with others was beautiful.

I still shiver when I think about it. Having an opportunity to bond with her and have fun with her was an extraordinary experience for me.

While Antarctica is the most remote place on the planet, it isn't the most untouched. According to a State of the Environment report, climate change poses the greatest threat to Antarctica, as opposed to the other continents. Because it is unpopulated, it is off the radar for most of us. But in some ways, it is the canary in the mine. In Antartica, 2,700 billion tonnes of ice were lost between 1992 and 2010, contributing to eight millimetres of sea level rise. What is even more unsettling is the fact that the speed of this loss has quadrupled in the last two decades. In 2023, Antarctica's sea ice reached its lowest level ever for the second year in a row. At 1.79 million square kilometres, it was 40 percent smaller than average between 1981 and 2010. Sea ice plays a key role in regulating Earth's climate.

We were there for five days. It is an extraordinary place. The icebergs are otherworldly. We plunged into the ocean, jumping off the ship into the frigid, minus-one-degree-Celsius water. We hiked on the continent, but the most impressive way to see Antarctica is by sea kayak. It was amazing, moving silently along the Antarctic coast, past sea lions, penguins, whales, and the massive ghostly icebergs floating by. We saw a leopard seal devouring a penguin. I felt like I was in the middle of the circle of life: the glaciers calve off into the ocean with their red algae; the red algae feeds the krill; the krill feeds the penguins, whales, and fish; the leopard seals eat the penguins; and the birds eat the leftovers. A sense of life at its simplest, raw and beautiful, without humans.

On the ship, we heard educational talks by various experts on the birds and mammals. But it was the ship's geologist who made the biggest impression on me. He explained that the

We plunged into the ocean, jumping off the ship into the frigid, minus-one-degree-Celsius water.

———————

continents will likely shift over the next 250 million years, forming a single supercontinent, like Pangaea. I asked him about saving the planet. He said the planet didn't need saving, that it will be fine for millions and millions of years to come. It was fine for the 4.5 billion years before we arrived, and it will be fine after we're gone. It will naturally regenerate in a rather short period of time after humans are gone. Saving the planet is just human ego; the thing we are really trying to save is ourselves, humanity.

Sitting in my kayak, in the midst of this extraordinary beauty, I thought about the Earth and humanity. The Earth would be beautiful without humans. And this observation raised difficult questions. Am I a parasite taking advantage of the world, or am I going to live a more sustainable life? The Earth will survive without us; it would likely flourish without us. But while we're here, how do I evolve and create space to appreciate and be part of honouring and sustaining its beauty?

Antarctica was a revelation. I returned home refreshed and filled with a renewed sense of purpose and curiosity. I was grateful for the time to reflect on my journey and what it meant to me. It meant reconciliation with my parents. A deeper recognition of their struggles, of the burdens they brought with them, of the grief they inherited. I have a greater understanding of my grandparents and the war that destroyed their lives and so much else. And I have reconciled with my former self: the curious child, the dyslexic student, the conflicted adolescent, that person sitting in the back of a car rambling along rural roads, drinking beer and listening to discussions about sex, not understanding how to fit in or even where to fit in.

Working through deep struggles, I finally had the answers to questions that had been lurking below the surface for all of my life. Do men feel the way I do? Why do I relate more to women? Why am I so drawn to beauty and feminine things, and where does my sensitivity and empathy come from? Questions that got louder and louder as I got older. Questions I tried to outrun with my commitment to building the so-called perfect life.

My thirty-year marriage had ended, a very difficult experience for everyone in my family. And my thirty-year career at the bank had come to a close, an incredible career that had consumed me. There was suddenly a vast, empty space. Facing the future as my authentic self, I had never felt more joy, awe, and freedom. I was learning to be free and me in the world.

At the same time, I was filled with fear and uncertainty. While I was beginning to attain an inner peace, my external fears remained. My journey forward meant tearing down more walls and biases I had built for my own protection and rebuilding myself through the lens of my inner child. I needed to remember the things I had done innately, out of joy and curiosity, not the things that I had done to fit into the world. I needed to heal and develop the mindfulness skills that would allow me to connect more deeply to my essence, my soul.

During the pandemic, I had the opportunity to spend time with Dr. Edith Eger, Holocaust survivor, psychologist, and author. I asked her how she handles her trauma and pain when it re-emerges. She said, "I sit with it and let it out... You're ready when you're ready, when something inside shifts and you decide. Until now you did that. Now [you're] going to do something else."

This period also created the space for me to grieve the many changes in my life, and to reconnect and reintegrate with the first fifty years of my life. When I first came out as Katie, there was a natural pull toward all that was female and feminine in me, and a push away from all that was male and masculine. I had become more mindful, practising meditation, letting grief emerge and flow, and letting it go. Over the course of a year, I experienced events that challenged me deeply.

I had a mental image of myself as a four-year-old child, an experience that carried hurt that I ultimately had not faced. I went looking for a photograph of my four-year-old self and ended up looking through fifty years of photos. There were pictures and experiences I had avoided for close to a decade. I wept steadily for hours as I sat with these memories, realizing aspects of my life I had tried to forget—even the hard ones when I was finally able to see an incredibly beautiful life. I'd had a wonderful life in a man's world, and now I had a beautiful life as all of me, as a woman, in a woman's world. I was able to see how each of these images and experiences were part of me, part of the whole human being I was today.

My journey has given me a perspective on the world that I could never have imagined. I feel able to appreciate and embrace all of the experiences and aspects of my life that have shaped me. My life in both a woman's and man's world, the outpouring of stories from around the world from colleagues, friends who enriched my understanding of humanity. It is those stories—of abuse, fear, shame, mental illness, poverty, different lived experiences... the stories we usually keep to ourselves—that give us the greatest understanding of what humanity actually is, the challenges others face, the secrets others carry. It isn't easy to share these histories and fears, but we need to see and understand them before we can move forward as individuals, as corporations, as a society.

So after more than a seven-year journey that involved my deepest sadness and my greatest joy, I knew there was something else I needed to do. Like other minorities— whether racial, gender, sexual, neurodiverse, persons with disabilities—I had concerns about how the world would greet me. But I wanted to go out into the world as Katie, to live my life and career as Katie, as Katherine. Today, the world gets all of me.

A dear friend, Annka Kultys, owns an art gallery in East London that focuses on exhibitions and storytelling through digital and contemporary art. Annka has been on her own beautiful journey, including living across Poland, Switzerland, France, and finally England, ultimately living her bliss and building her gallery. She is inspiring on many levels, and speaks of living in her *truth*, *vision*, and *exhibition*, or curation.

I bring into this next chapter of my life my own *truth* and *vision*. My truth and essence. My lived experiences and a deep curiosity for and love of our world, and a love of humanity and the incredible good I know we are capable of. A vision centred on helping unlock human potential through inclusivity and a shared sense of kindness, empathy, and connection; defining and building leadership capabilities of the future; and building sustainable organizations. The curation of this next chapter will play out over time. I want to be of service, and to help build the kinder, more inclusive and sustainable society and world we desire.

Canadian environmental activist David Suzuki said something decades ago that has shaped and impacted me deeply. He said that we are each grains of sand with each step or action we take. Each action we take adds to the sand hill. You don't know whether or not you are the grain of sand that causes the land slide of change. You just know that each grain of sand matters equally, each person and each action matters equally. It's all that has ever mattered.

We're given one life. I want to experience and help care for this extraordinary world in all its beauty and fullness.

As I move fully into this next phase, I feel free and full of love, hope, and faith. I feel inspired. My friend Dr. Robyne

Hanley-Dafoe does extraordinary work in the wellness, resilience, and mental wellness space. In a meeting on March 6, 2023, she said to me, "Katie, if we as individuals have a unique skill or perspective in this world of eight billion people, it is our obligation to share it with others for the greater good. This world needs more hope."

If this book saves one life, or helps one child, parent, or leader be better, kinder, or more impactful, I will be forever grateful.

Epilogue

Awe is the feeling of being in the presence
of something vast that transcends your
current understanding of the world.

DACHER KELTNER

AS 2021 WAS COMING TO A CLOSE, I met an extraordinary woman. I had given my friend, Andreas, a shopping list of everything I was looking for in a friend; I preferred them to be independent, strong, loving, kind, intelligent, open-minded, feminine, curious, and playful. A week later, he said he had the perfect person for me, an Athena. (He understands what I mean when I use that term.) I immediately reached out to her and we met at a French restaurant in Toronto's Distillery District. Our dinner lasted almost six hours. We shared life stories—beautiful stories and hard ones. We shared passions, interests, and hopes for the future. We developed an immediate and deep connection. The feeling of being seen, heard, and appreciated fully by someone so special helped me see, understand, and love myself.

In the spring of 2022, my friend and I took a trip to Italy, starting in Venice. I wore my brown and white polka-dot dress—the dress worn by Vivian, played by Julia Roberts, in *Pretty Woman* thirty years earlier. I had always wanted to make an *Eat Pray Love*–style trip. And now I was doing it—me, Katherine.

We hiked in the Dolomite Mountains. The rolling alpine meadows were filled with wildflowers. There was a small herd of horses, and I watched a horse and her foal break away from the group and begin walking toward us. The mare was a gorgeous tan colour with a white star above her nose; her foal had a matching star. They kept walking toward us, toward me. The horse lowered her head and put the white star in the palm of my hand. I could feel the mare's gentle heart and compassion. I wept and spoke to her quietly. I was in awe. Never before has a horse, or any animal for that matter, approached me in such a way. The two horses stayed with us for what felt like an eternity.

The weather was glorious. The sun shone and a few white clouds hovered over the peaks. It occurred to me that my father might have come through here on his motorcycle a lifetime ago. It may have been the happiest time in his life. Certainly, it was when he was most free. He had always been imprisoned by something—the German army, brutal Russians, hunger, poverty, the responsibility of a family. But for this brief moment, he would have been unencumbered, the wind in his hair, his life filled with possibility.

In awe, with my heart fully open, I felt alive and free—ready for what was to come. Cows dotted the meadows, grazing freely, more than a hundred of them. My dear friend and I were both moved to tears by the beauty and the soft tinkling of dozens of cowbells. Standing there in my truth and full of love, I thought, *I'm free. I'm home.*

Acknowledgements

T HIS BOOK is a tribute to the thousands of individuals, including family, friends, colleagues, mentors, coaches, guides, and many more, who have believed in me, supported me, loved me, encouraged me, and urged me to share my journey and insights. I am here today because of you—because you gave me the care, kindness, love, support, embrace, insight, and strength I needed when I could not find it in myself. You have done the same for my family.

I am beyond grateful for and moved beyond words by those closest to me:

To Rosemary and our incredible four children: You were most impacted by my truth and the many challenges and changes that followed. You gave me purpose and strength. Together, we tackled another "Dudtschak Adventure" with grit, love, honesty, and determination.

Mona and Becky, we have lived this entire lifetime together. Our love has been a constant through each and every experience along the way. And you embraced me as your sister from the first second. I wish Mom and Dad could see in person the extraordinary daughters they gave life to, raised, and gave purpose to. They are watching with all of the love of the universe and beyond.

To Lee Anne and Mike, Bob and Janice, Nancy and Rob, George, Monica, and Jaime: You and many more have been the core of "Team Dudtschak" and "Team Katie" from the first moment you heard my truth. We shared tears, and you immediately moved to provide the encouragement, hope, and inspiration that Rosemary, the kids, and I needed to navigate this road. You have given me confidence, courage, and strength at the most critical of times.

Laura, from the first moment we connected and shared life stories, I felt a special connection. You inspired me. I felt seen, heard, understood, and cared for with a depth and in ways I had never experienced. You helped me see and love myself. You are truly extraordinary and a gift from the universe. You connected with and touched my soul at the deepest level.

Thank you, Don Gillmor, for your editorial help, and Michael Levine, for your guidance with this project. Thank you to everyone on the Page Two publishing team.

A portion of the proceeds from this book will be donated to Incluvest Foundation, which is dedicated to unlocking human potential to solve humanity's greatest challenges. To learn more, visit torontofoundation.ca/incluvest-foundation.

Notes

Introduction

p. 3   Epigraph: Betty Sue Flowers in Joseph Jaworski, *Synchronicity: The Inner Path of Leadership* (Berrett-Koehler Publishers, 1996), 195.

p. 6   *Bohm envisioned a society*: Wikipedia, "Bohm Dialogue," last modified December 1, 2024, 15:14 (UTC), en.wikipedia.org/wiki/Bohm_Dialogue.

Chapter 1

p. 9   Epigraph: Nikita Gill, "Stop Looking Behind You," Thought Catalog, June 4, 2016, thoughtcatalog.com/nikita-gill/2016/05/stop-looking-behind-you.

Chapter 2

p. 29   Epigraph: Bianca Sparacino, *The Strength in Our Scars* (Thought Catalog Books, 2018).

p. 30   *"politically unreliable"*: United States Holocaust Memorial Museum, "Antisemitic Legislation 1933–1939," USHMM, *Holocaust Encyclopedia*, encyclopedia.ushmm.org/content/en/article/antisemitic-legislation -1933-1939.

p. 30   *Gay men were being arrested:* Wikipedia, "Persecution of Homosexuals in Nazi Germany," last modified April 24, 2025, 12:33 (UTC), en.wikipedia .org/wiki/Persecution_of_homosexuals_in_Nazi_Germany.

p. 31   *"Here was an entire nation"*: Thomas Wolfe quoted in Erik Larson, *In the Garden of the Beasts: Love, Terror and an American Family in Hitler's Berlin* (Crown Publishers, 2011), 223.

p. 31   *Canadian Prime Minister William Lyon Mackenzie King:* "Rise of Hitler," *Canada: A People's History*, CBC, cbc.ca/history /EPISCONTENTSE1EP13CH4PA1LE.html.

p. 31 *Canada's military and government:* Ron Levy, "Canada's Cold War Purge of 2SLGBTQ+ from Public Service," *Canadian Encyclopedia*, October 3, 2018, updated by Andrew McIntosh, April 17, 2025, thecanadianencyclopedia.ca/en/article/lgbtq-purge-in-canada.

p. 31 *September 1, 1939:* Christopher Klein, "How Germany's Invasion of Poland Kicked Off WWII," History, updated February 19, 2025, history.com/articles/world-war-ii-begins-german-invasion-poland-1939.

p. 32 *The Germans rolled:* Thomas A. Hughes and John Graham Royd-Smith, "The Germans' Summer Offensive in Southern Russia, 1942," *Britannica*, April 29, 2025, britannica.com/event/World-War-II/The-Germans-summer-offensive-in-southern-Russia-1942.

p. 32 *a humiliating defeat:* Christoph Hasselbach, "The Battle of Stalingrad: A Decisive Turning Point in WW2," February 2, 2023, DW (Deutche Welle), dw.com/en/the-battle-of-stalingrad-a-decisive-turning-point-in-ww2/a-42344954.

Chapter 3
p. 45 Epigraph: Rick Warren, Twitter (now X), April 15, 2011, x.com/RickWarren/status/59006112120315904.

Chapter 4
p. 63 Epigraph: Brené Brown, *The Gifts of Imperfection* (Hazelden, 2010), xxvi.

p. 64 *with the cover line:* See *National Geographic*, Gender Revolution special issue, January 2017, nationalgeographic.com/magazine/issue/january-2017.

p. 74 *More than half of 2SLGBTQ+:* Rina Torchinsky, "Nearly Half of LGBTQ Youth Seriously Considered Suicide, Survey Finds," NPR, Special Series: Efforts to Restrict Rights for LGBTQ Youth, May 5, 2022, npr.org/2022/05/05/1096920693/lgbtq-youth-thoughts-of-suicide-trevor-project-survey.

p. 75 *In her 1974 memoir:* Jan Morris, *Conundrum* (NYRB Classics, 2016), 25.

Chapter 5
p. 87 Epigraph: Ash Alves, quoted on Powerful Women Pray's website under their download "Speak Life: Powerful Faith-Filled Affirmations for Every Season," powerfulwomenpray.com/products/speak-life-powerful-faith-filled-affirmations-for-every-season.

p. 88   *"Who looks outside"*: C.G. Jung, *C.G. Jung Letters, Vol. 2*. (Princeton University Press, Bollingen Series, 1976), 363.

p. 102   *found a link between:* Axenya Kachen and Jennifer R. Pharr, "Health Care Access and Utilization by Transgender Populations: A United States Transgender Survey Study," *Journal of the American Medical Association* 5, no. 3 (2020): 141–48, doi.org/10.1089/trgh.2020.0017.

p. 103   *more and more US states:* "State Legislators Propose 300 Anti-LGBTQ Bill as GLAAD Releases Updated Reporter Guide, Resources," GLAAD, February 10, 2023, glaad.org/releases/state-legislators-propose-300-anti-lgbtq-bills-glaad-releases-updated-reporter-guide.

p. 104   *In the movie: Eat Pray Love*, directed by Ryan Murphy (Culver City, CA: Columbia Pictures, Plan B Entertainment, and Sony Pictures Releasing, 2010).

Chapter 6

p. 107   Epigraph: Joseph Campbell, *Companion: Reflections on the Art of Living* (Harper, 1992) ; *Joseph Campbell and the Power of Myth*, episode 6, "Masks of Eternity," aired June 26, 1988, on PBS.

p. 109   *"Opportunities to find":* "Joseph Campbell Quotes," Goodreads, goodreads.com/quotes/230531-opportunities-to-find-deeper-powers-within-ourselves-come-when-life.

p. 111   *One of the people:* Interview with "Mary," InclusionDialogues, April 4, 2023.

p. 114   *The first residential:* J.R. Miller, "Residential Schools in Canada," *Canadian Encyclopedia*, updated by Tabitha De Bruin, David Gallant, and Michelle Filice, January 11, 2024, thecanadianencyclopedia.ca/en/article/residential-schools.

p. 115   *Kivalliq Hall:* "The Significance of the IRSSA-Recognized Schools in Indigenous Relations," Indigenous Corporate Training Inc., September 17, 2024, ictinc.ca/blog/the-significance-of-irssa-recognized-schools-in-indigenous-relations.

p. 115   *more than five thousand*: Martha Troian, "Indian Residential Schools: 5,300 Alleged Abusers Located by Ottawa," CBC News, February 2, 2016, cbc.ca/news/indigenous/residential-school-alleged-abusers-iap-1.3422770.

p. 118   *"Susan's" story:* Interview with "Susan," InclusionDialogues, April 21, 2023.

p. 122   *Another story came:* Interviews with "Robert," InclusionDialogues, March 19, 2023, and April 27, 2023.

p. 124   *I connected with:* Interview with "Marieke," InclusionDialogues, May 9, 2023.

p. 129   *"disorienting dilemmas":* Jack Mezirow, *Transformative Dimensions of Adult Learning* (Jossey-Bass, 1991).

p. 129   *"Wisdom without compassion":* Fred Kofman, "How to Bring Wisdom and Compassion to the Business World (Wisdom and Compassion, Part 1.1)," LinkedIn article, June 29, 2015, linkedin.com/pulse /how-bring-wisdom-compassion-business-world-part-11-fred-kofman. He also included a version of this idea in his book *Conscious Business: How to Build Value Through Values* (Sounds True, 2013).

Chapter 7

p. 131   Epigraph: Glenn Close, *Bring Change to Mind, Let's Talk Mental Health: Impact Report,* assets.bringchange2mind.org/wp-content/uploads /20181225010924/bc2m-impact-report-v6c.pdf.

p. 132   *Canada has the third-highest:* For Canadian suicide statistics, see "Suicide in Canada," Mental Health and Wellness, Suicide Prevention, Government of Canada, canada.ca/en/public-health/services/suicide-prevention /suicide-canada.html.

p. 133   *handled 4.6 million calls:* Kids Help Phone facts can be found on their website. See, for example, kidshelpphone.ca/get-involved/kids-face -grown-up-problems-we-can-all-support-them; kidshelpphone.ca/get -insights/home#data-impact; and kidshelpphone.ca/get-info/2slgbtq -youth-allies-this-is-your-space.

p. 137   *"If you had asked":* Eric Windeler, in discussion with the author, March 2023.

p. 139   *70 percent of mental illness: Campus Assessment Tool Report 2024,* jack.org, 2024, assets.jack.org/m/566b45bf7d8f7919/original/2024 -CAT-Report-V4.pdf.

p. 139   *worked at the Centre:* Mary Deacon, in discussion with the author, March 2023.

p. 142   *seriously considered suicide:* The Trevor Project, "2022 National Survey on LGBTQ Youth Mental Health," thetrevorproject.org/survey-2022.

p. 143   *"war against 2SLGBTQ+":* "Under Fire Series: The War on LGBTQ People in America," Movement Advancement Project (MAP), 2023, mapresearch .org/under-fire-report.

p. 143   *A significant percentage:* Jody L. Herman, Andrew R. Flores, and Kathryn O'Neill, *How Many Adults and Youth Identify as Transgender in the United States?* UCLA School of Law Williams Institute report, June 2022, williamsinstitute.law.ucla.edu/publications/trans-adults -united-states.

p. 144 *"Being able to be"*: I can no longer find the source of this quotation, but it is often posted on social media and on websites, and is attributed to Dr. Lauren Fogel Mersy, a psychologist, sex therapist, and couples therapist. Her website is drlaurenfogel.com.

p. 144 *first public transgender*: Christine Jorgensen, *Christine Jorgensen: A Personal Autobiography* (Cleis Press, 2000).

p. 144 *Ninety-six percent*: Equality Forum, with Louis Thomas and Ian Ayres, "Forbes 500 Non-Discrimination Project," Equality Forum, equalityforum.com/fortune500.

p. 146 *the Liberal government*: "Canada Is the First Country to Provide Census Data on Transgender and Non-Binary People," *The Daily*, Statistics Canada, April 27, 2022, www150.statcan.gc.ca/n1/daily-quotidien/220427/dq220427b-eng.htm.

p. 148 *there were 1.9 million interactions*: Black Press Media Staff, "Kids Help Phone Aims to Raise Record $300M to Expand Virtual Mental Health Care," *The Abbotsford News*, March 3, 2023, abbynews.com/news/kids-help-phone-aims-to-raise-record-300m-to-expand-virtual-mental-health-care-1833928; Kids Help Phone team and Kathy Hay in discussion with the author, 2022.

p. 148 *Research has shown*: Jacob Stokl, Jenny Hui, Shelley Craig, "Affirming 2SLGBTQ+ Children and Youth in Child Welfare: Key Challenges and Practice Opportunities," Homeless Hub, June 28, 2024, homelesshub.ca/blog/2024/affirming-2slgbtq-children-and-youth-child-welfare-key-challenges-and-practice-opportunities.

p. 149 *Outside of their home*: "Being Safe, Being Me: Results of the Canadian Trans Youth Health Survey," Stigma and Resilience Among Vulnerable Youth Centre (SARAVYC), May 6, 2018, saravyc.ubc.ca/2018/05/06/trans-youth-health-survey.

p. 149 *a psychiatrist at CAMH*: Dr. June Lam, in discussion with the author, April 2023.

p. 150 *one of the most protective*: Greta R. Bauer et al., "Intervenable Factors Associated with Suicide Risk in Transgender Persons: A Respondent Driven Sampling Study in Ontario, Canada," *BMC Public Health* 15, art. no. 525 (2015): doi.org/10.1186/s12889-015-1867-2.

Chapter 8

p. 155 Epigraph: Eckhart Tolle, *A New Earth: Awakening to Your Life's Purpose* (Penguin Life, 2005), 106.

p. 157 *Director Greta Gerwig*: *Barbie*, directed by Greta Gerwig (Burbank, CA: Warner Bros., 2023).

p. 158   *Research showed that:* Supriya Garikipati and Uma Kambhampati, "Leading the Fight Against the Pandemic: Does Gender Really Matter?" *Feminist Economics* 27, nos. 1–2 (2021): 401–18, doi.org/10.1080 /13545701.2021.1874614.

p. 158   *leadership effectiveness ratings:* Jack Zenger and Joseph Folkman, "Research: Women Are Better Leaders During a Crisis," *Harvard Business Review,* December 30, 2020, hbr.org/2020/12/research-women-are -better-leaders-during-a-crisis.

p. 161   *I reached out:* Betty Sue Flowers, in discussion with the author, virtual, October 20, 2020.

p. 167   *"Education is the most":* Nelson Mandela, address at the launch of Mindset Network in Johannesburg, South Africa, July 16, 2003, mandela.gov.za /mandela_speeches/2003/030716_mindset.htm.

Chapter 9

p. 169   Epigraph: Rachel Gillett, "'The World Is Full of Monsters': Steven Spielberg Tells Harvard Grads to Fight Injustice and 'Create a World That Lasts Forever,'" *Business Insider,* May 16, 2016, businessinsider.com /steven-spielberg-harvard-commencement-speech-2016-5.

p. 169   *"We are asleep":* Bill Marriott, "Waiting for a Wake Up Call," Dr. John Izzo, *Purpose Revolution* (blog), November 26, 2014, drjohnizzo.com /purpose-blog/change-management/waiting-for-a-wake-up-call.

p. 169   *in June 2023:* Nouran Salahieh, Joe Sutton, and Lauren Mascarenhas, "More Than a Third of the US Population, from the Midwest to the East Coast, Under Air Quality Alerts from Canadian Wildfire Smoke," CNN, June 28, 2023, cnn.com/2023/06/27/us/canada-wildfire-smoke-great -lakes/index.html.

p. 170   *competing individual interests:* Garrett Hardin, "The Tragedy of the Commons," *Science* 162, no. 3859 (1968), 1243–48, doi.org/10.1126 /science.162.3859.1243.

p. 171   *"I travelled extensively":* Phil Fontaine, in discussion with the author, June 20, 2023.

p. 179   *Approximately 25 percent:* "Dyslexic Entrepreneurs Are Successful by Any Measure. It's All in the Way We Think," Gershoni Creative, n.d., gershoni. com/culture/dyslexic-entrepreneurs-are-successful-by-any-measure; Louis Ricci, "Dyslexia and ADHD: What's the Connection?" Exceptional Individuals, February 6, 2023, exceptionalindividuals.com /about-us/blog/dyslexia-and-adhd-whats-the-connection.

p. 182 *"Failure isn't a necessary"*: Ed Catmull with Amy Wallace, *Creativity Inc:
Overcoming the Unseen Forces that Stand in the Way of True Inspiration*
(Random House, 2023), Introduction.

p. 187 *"Government really sets"*: John Izzo, in discussion with the author,
June 12, 2023.

p. 189 *transformational learning*: Mezirow, *Transformative Dimensions*.

p. 190 *I asked her how*: Corie Barry speaking at a women's program, March 2021.

p. 190 *the myths of leadership*: Hubert Joly, *The Heart of Business* (Harvard
Business Review Press, 2021).

p. 192 *introduction of required learning*: See Reconciliation Education,
reconciliationeducation.ca/en-ca.

Chapter 10

p. 199 Epigraph: Charlotte Eriksson, "I'm Trying, as I Always Will," in
Everything Changed When I Forgave Myself (Broken Glass Records, 2018),
charlotteeriksson.com/post/tryingasialwayswill.

p. 202 *climate change poses*: "Climate Change Poses Greatest Threat to
Antarctica," Australian Government, Australian Antarctic Program,
July 20, 2022, antarctica.gov.au/news/2022/climate-change-poses
-greatest-threat-to-antarctica.

p. 205 *how she handles*: Dr. Edith Eger, in discussion with the author, June 17,
2021. Edith was a guest speaker at a women's executive learning forum
held by World 50.

p. 207 *we are each grains*: The actual quotation is: "In *Earth in the Balance*,
Al Gore described the results of research on the physical properties of
growing sandpiles. When grains of sand are added to a pile one at a time,
the pile grows until it reaches a critical point at which the addition of one
more grain of sand causes avalanches, slides and massive changes. It is an
apt metaphor for the way individuals can create sudden shifts in popular
understanding and social action. No one can predict when that critical
point can be reached when one additional grain can be the final agent that
will cause an enormous shift. Each person, group or organization working
towards a different world may seem powerless and insignificant, but all
of them can add up to a force that can become irresistible." David Suzuki,
The Sacred Balance (Greystone Books, 1999), n.p.

Epilogue

p. 209 Epigraph: Dachner Keltner, *Awe: The New Science of Everyday Wonder and
How It Can Transform Your Life* (Penguin Press, 2023), 7.

About the Author

KATHERINE DUDTSCHAK has worked for over thirty years as one of Canada's most recognized and respected CEOs and business leaders with extensive financial services skills and experience. Having affirmed her gender in 2019, Katherine has lived in both a man's world and woman's world and intimately understands the challenges of each one. She acts as a bridge between divides, using her experience and voice to advocate for and advance a truly kind, inclusive, and sustainable world.

Katherine is an advocate, thought leader, and community builder, having dedicated her volunteer efforts to causes in the areas of sustainability, next-generation leadership, human rights, poverty prevention, mental wellness and health, immigration, Indigenous reconciliation, education, economic development, and arts and culture. She is also the founder of Incluvest Foundation, dedicated to unlocking human potential to solve humanity's greatest challenges, and defining and advancing leadership for a truly harmonious and sustainable world.

Katherine grew up on a small farm to newcomer parents who survived WWII refugee and prisoner camps. She is the mother of four wonderful children.

For media inquiries,
speaking engagements,
collaborations, or to learn more,
visit sincerelykatherine.com.